Psychology for the Classroom: E-Learning

John Woollard

 Routledge
Taylor & Francis Group

LONDON AND NEW YORK

First published 2011
by Routledge
2 Park Square, Milton Park, Abingdon, Oxon OX14 4RN

Simultaneously published in the USA and Canada
by Routledge
711 Third Avenue, New York, NY 10017

Routledge is an imprint of the Taylor & Francis Group, an informa business

British Library Cataloguing in Publication Data
A catalogue record for this book is available from the British Library

Library of Congress Cataloging-in-Publication Data
Woollard, John, author.
Psychology for the classroom: E-learning / By John Woollard.— First edition.
    pages; cm
Includes bibliographical references and index.
1. Computer-assisted instruction. 2. Educational psychology. I. Title.
LB1028.5.W627 2011
371.33'4019—dc22   2010042300

ISBN13: 978–0–415–59092–1 (hbk)
ISBN13: 978–0–415–59093–8 (pbk)
ISBN13: 978–0–203–81916–6 (ebk)

Typeset in Bembo by
Book Now Ltd, London
Printed and bound in Great Britain by
CPI Antony Rowe, Chippenham, Wiltshire

Contents

List of illustrations   vii
Series preface   ix
Acknowledgements   xiii
Contributors   xv

1   Introduction   1
    Towards a definition of e-learning   2
    Changing thinking: changing the ways of learning   4
    A brief history of technology-enabled learning   8
    Pedagogy, andragogy and cybergogy   11
    Mapping the psychology   13

2   Research   19
    Online learning: a meta-analysis of research   20
    Collaborative and social learning   24
    Using ICT to support teaching   30
    Technology-mediated learning   34
    E-safety in e-learning: safe-working in the virtual world   37

3   Theory   45
    Stages of cognitive development   45
    An educational software paradigm   52
    Stages of online interactivity   54
    Learning in cyberspace   56
    ID, Id, avatar and persona: the changing face of self   58

4   Pedagogy   67
     Using learning technologies   68
     Using virtual learning environments   81
     Cybergogy: learning in virtual worlds   90

5   Strategy   95
     Strategies of the technology-enabled teacher   96
     Computer-mediated collaboration   97
     Sustained online learning   100
     Teaching in the virtual world   103
     Using authoring to increase learner engagement   106
     Professionals learning in the virtual world   109
     E-safety in learning and teaching   113

References   119
Index   133

Illustrations

Figures

0.1	The conceptual path taken by each author when writing	xi
1.1	The three components of e-learning	4
1.2	The range and diversity of technology-enabled learning	7
1.3	The changing face of learning	14
1.4	Mapping the psychology of e-learning	15
1.5	Analysing the psychological dimension of e-resources	16
2.1	The cognitive/social asynchronous/synchronous dimensions of learning	23
2.2	Examples of activities enhanced by computer-supported collaboration	25
2.3	The life of a thread – key points in the chronology	26
2.4	Promoting participation and interaction	28
2.5	Questioning learners regarding the technology	36
3.1	Reflections of a six-year-old on using a Roamer	48
3.2	ReTreeval software for creating tree data structures	49
3.3	Using technology to explore proportion more thoroughly	50
3.4	Scattergram showing the relationship between two values from each member of a set	51
3.5	The three functions of avatars	59
3.6	Classical hierarchical diagram	60
4.1	Pedagogy arising through theory, policy (politics) and practice	68
4.2	Hierarchy of engagement	75
4.3	Routes of communication	85
5.1	Three contrasting peregrination choices	112
5.2	Essential elements of acceptable use policies	117

Tables

1.1	What is e-learning?	3
2.1	Synchronous and asynchronous online learning opportunities	22
2.2	Measuring engagement in threaded discussions – the degree of social construction	27
3.1	Stages of cognitive development	46
3.2	Five-stage model of learning and socialisation in a virtual world	56
3.3	Terminology of cybergogy	57
3.4	Moral development and response to ethics in learning environments	62
3.5	Traits of personality of the Big Five taxonomy	64
4.1	Analysis of critical thinking	77
4.2	Mindtools – functions and examples	77
4.3	The Six Hats and e-learning skills	79
4.4	Learning platform architecture and learning processes	83
4.5	Teaching strategies and learning technologies	84
4.6	Types of assessment: baseline, formative (diagnostic), ipsative and summative	88
4.7	Peer-assessment and self-assessment	89
4.8	Forms of assessment	89
4.9	The learning domains of cybergogy	91
4.10	The learning archetypes with frames and sub-frames	93
4.11	The levels of implementation for the domains of learning	93
4.12	Exemplification of a learning activity within the social domain	94
5.1	Content, contact and conduct aspects of e-safety	116
5.2	'Click Clever Click Safe' campaign, UK Council for Child Internet Safety	117

Series preface

The focus of this series of books is the psychological elements of educational practice. The series aims to draw together and elucidate, at more than a superficial level, the major current topics of concern that are related to learning and to other important areas of psychological interest.

In the past, teachers in training were introduced, at an entry level at least, to some of the psychology of learning and education. Although this element of the United Kingdom teacher training curriculum (TDA, 2008) has not quite disappeared completely, there is a considerably reduced emphasis placed on it in teacher training than previously. Teachers currently in post report that they were not introduced satisfactorily to what they consider important aspects of learning, theory in particular, during their training (Pritchard, 2005). The relative success of *Ways of Learning* (Pritchard, 2005; 2009), and other books dealing with the same subject matter, can be seen as indicative of a need for more psychology for teachers and teachers in training.

In support of the wider rationale for the series, the work of Burton and Bartlett (2006: 44–45) has some important points to make. They suggest that there is a danger that new ideas for pedagogical approaches in the classroom are often promoted, sometimes by government agencies, without the detailed research and theoretical underpinning relating to it being considered due diligence: 'The speed with which the internet and television can transmit ideas and information and appear to afford them (often spurious) validation should concern us as educators' (44). They are concerned that, 'high-profile education consultants deliver courses on new pedagogies' (45). These presentations are 'drawn eclectically from a range of research findings thought to have practical benefits for learning' (45) and that teachers 'generally enjoy these stimulating sessions and the recipe approach to pedagogic techniques but they are not encouraged to look deeper into the research that underpins them' (45). The books in this series aim to provide the opportunity, in an accessible and relevant way, to enable teachers, teachers in training and others with a professional interest in children, classrooms and learning, to look more deeply at topics, their background research and potential efficacy, and to be able to make choices about their own pedagogical approaches and preferences from a position of knowledge and understanding. The authors will consider the needs of those in training, following courses that expect the detailed presentation of ideas at master's level, giving leads to follow, ideas to develop and exemplary writing of professional and academic quality. This is important, as it is increasingly the case that courses leading to Qualified Teacher Status (QTS) in the UK are linking assessed work to master's level expectations and awarding credits towards master's degrees. This is particularly the case with postgraduate level teacher training courses.

The series, in turn, presents and examines the detail and potential of a range of psychology-related topics in the light of their value and usefulness for practising teachers. Each of the authors presents an outline of the topic, a review of the research which underpins its principles, the implications of the underpinning theory for pedagogy and, lastly, a consideration of strategies which teachers might employ if they were to wish to implement the precepts of theory in their teaching. The books aim to outline a trail from research and theory, to pedagogy and, thence, to teaching strategies in practice. There is a clear pedagogical element to the books, presenting the ideas in the perspectives of research, theory, pedagogy and strategies for teaching. There are suggestions for further reading and activities, both written, to develop understanding, and classroom-based, to develop skills and knowledge. The more general strategies will provide teachers with sound starting points for developing their own particular plans for lessons and series of lessons, including activities which will be informed by the principles of the topic in question.

Research is presented and explored, the theory generated by the research is outlined and the pedagogical implications of the theory, leading to teaching strategies follow. Within a set, but flexible, framework individual authors have written in a way suited both to them and to the topic in question.

Part of the intention of the series is to look beyond the charisma of the presenters of day courses, and similar, for teachers (Burton and Bartlett, 2006) and beyond the showy, commercialised publications aimed at selling expensive materials. Each book aims to give an evidence-based consideration of the possibilities afforded by new findings and ideas, and give a review of research upon which claims for teaching efficacy have been built and a solid foundation for teachers and those in training to build their own ideas and strategies. The new ideas and findings are presented in the context of existing knowledge, understanding and practice of the topic in question.

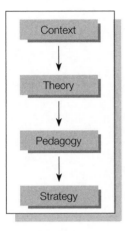

Figure 0.1 The conceptual path taken by each author when writing

Acknowledgements

I would like to say thanks to the colleagues and students who have enhanced my experiences and influenced my views during the previous 32 years of using computers in my teaching. Working at the leading edge of educational innovation can be challenging, for the learners as well as the teachers, and so, to my pupils and students, I am particularly grateful. Special thanks go to: Andy Neil, Catherine Richards, Ce Amey, Claire Johnson, Fengyin Lin, Gill Piper, Lesley Scopes, Mariam Mohamad and Tamer Abd El-Gawad, who have influenced my thinking in these matters.

This book is dedicated to my wife, Heather.

John Woollard
September 2010

Contributors

Lesley Scopes completed her master's degree in computer-based learning and training at the University of Southampton with a dissertation 'Learning Archetypes as Tools of Cybergogy for 3D Educational Landscape: A Structure for eTeaching in Second Life'. She now teaches and trains in virtual world environments in the USA and the UK and presents her work in conventional and virtual world conferences. Catch up with her, as Light Sequent, on YouTube, blip.tv and Second Life®.

Tim Williams is Programme Leader (Work Centred Learning Programme) in the Faculty of Education at Anglia Ruskin University and has been part of the development of the Ultraversity online degree programme since its inception at UltraLab, Anglia Ruskin University, in 2003. He is now also involved in supporting faculties across the university as they develop online learning pathways based on the experience gained from Ultraversity. He is particularly interested in the new possibilities and implications for the use of technology in assessing students.

1 Introduction

By the end of the chapter you will be able to:

- recall the historical perspective of technology-enabled teaching and learning;
- understand the scope of technology-enabled learning and explain the terminology;
- define, in terms of your practice, the scope of technology-enabled teaching;
- understand the concept of e-learning (that is, the special form of learning only associated with the use of technology); and
- relate the key features of technology to the key areas of educational theory and psychology.

The developments in teaching and learning in the twenty-first century are growing more and more dependent upon web-based and computer-based technologies. Technology is having a positive impact upon learning: the ImpaCT2 study (DfES, 2002a) showed improved grades for school pupils; the ICT Test Bed programme (Somekh *et al.*, 2007) reported that learner satisfaction rose dramatically, with pupils showing greater independence in their learning; and students in UK further education showed better understanding and speedier progress through their courses (Finlayson *et al.*, 2006). These developments are presenting new opportunities, contexts and environments for learning. 'E-learning', as in the title of this book, encompasses the diverse range of theories and applied aspects of teaching and learning including: virtual learning environments, social networking, personalisation, social justice, cyber-bullying and e-safety, blended learning, avatars and virtual worlds, cybergogy and new learning domains, and so on. Indeed, the very letter 'e' is developing other meanings, such as 'e3-learning' (effective, efficient, and engaging learning) (Spector and Merrill, 2008).

This book, like others in the series, will follow the same format of exploring the research, presenting the theories, describing the pedagogy (and cybergogy) and illustrating with vignettes. First, there is an exploration of the scope and diversity within the field of e-learning and a definition of the terms that will be encountered.

Towards a definition of e-learning

E-learning is a complex construct of teaching and learning strategies, a way of organising the curriculum and a method of teaching. E-learning is also a learning theory identifying those aspects of knowing and understanding that relate to computers or occur as a direct result of the use of computers. Perceptions of e-learning amongst teachers, theorists and the public are varied and the socially constructed definition is continuing to form. The table on the following page illustrates the diversity, complexity and pervasive nature of e-learning.

It is evident that the world of e-learning is dominated by technical words, abbreviations and acronyms. This book endeavours both to explain and to rationalise the range and diversity of e-learning facilities, whether historical but with current relevance, or those in present use with significance for future e-learning practice. Because of the diverse and varied nature of e-learning activity, it is also likely that any single definition will omit or reduce in emphasis one or more aspects that other practitioners might deem important. However, an attempt at definition must be made.

For the purposes of the book, the working definition for e-learning is given below.

> E-learning is any form of teaching, training or tutoring designed to meet the needs of identified learners of any age and ability by scheduled or continual provision via the internet or mobile telephones, using electronic multimedia resources, computers and computer-based devices.

Table 1.1 What is e-learning?

what	is a form of teaching, training or tutoring;	CAL, CBL, CAI, CML, CBA, CAA;
	it is a technology for teaching;	IT, ICT, microcomputers, computers, PCs, laptops, web books, SMS, MMS;
	is a facilitator of learning;	MLE, VLE, PLE, LP, LMS, CMS, VIE, CMC, CSCL;
	sometimes through social interaction.	social site, profile, 3Di, VW, avatar.
who	is for learners of all ages;	two years and older, including the silver surfers;
	is for all abilities.	special educational needs to post-doctorate.
when	is always available; or	24-7, web pages, Web 2.0, wiki, blog, forum, Twitter™, email, RSS, podcasting;
	is scheduled and time structured.	webinar, videoconferencing, web conferences, chat, chat rooms, internet messenger, e-conferences, virtual worlds.
where	is everywhere, accessible by the internet;	WWW, email, IM, FTP, Available HTTPS, cloud technology, cyber-spaces;
	is also provided through resources; and/or	presentation files, pdf, CD, DVD, audio files (e.g. MP3), video files (e.g. MP4), SMS (text) and MMS (media message service);
	can be integrated with face-to-face teaching.	blended learning.
how	through a computer;	technology-enabled teaching, learning technologies, educational technology, technology-enhanced teaching;
	through other technologies such as ...	mobile-learning (m-learning), audio player, telephone, mobile telephone (GPRS/3G), internet-enabled mobile telephone, podcasting, vodcasting.
why	to enable personal advancement through informal engagement;	inclusion: accessibility, convenience, user-friendly;
	to support and complement formal tuition;	personalisation: student-centeredness, individualised,
	to provide just enough, just in time support;	learner-centred;
	to provide tuition that takes place away from the classroom;	open learning; life-long learning;
	to meet learner expectations.	financial expediency; efficiency; new markets.

The three essential components can be represented diagrammatically as:

the *action* of
for example, teaching, training or tutoring
by *means* of
a technology or technology-based resources
with the *intention* to
enable learners to learn
(skills, knowledge or understanding)

Figure 1.1 The three components of e-learning

This definition is broad so that it encompasses practices of the foreseeable future, as well as many of the practices involving the use of computers in education that have taken place over the previous 50 years. Many of those bygone activities have characteristics that remain valid today and, importantly, the underpinning *principles of psychology* remain valid. However, there is another meaning of e-learning; the next section explores the changing act of learning.

Changing thinking: changing the ways of learning

However, there is one meaning of e-learning that is very different from the definition above – it is where e-learning is the act of the learner to learn something in a specific way or of a specific type that is not the same as conventional learning.

> E-learning is different from ordinary learning.

This is a challenging concept and this definition of e-learning is one worthy of study and discussion. E-learning is learning that is different from any form of learning prior to the use of technology. The context for this discussion is emphatically expressed by Ian Jukes in his keynote presentation (Jukes, 2010), where he describes Marc Prensky's idea of digital natives and digital immigrants and how they show signs of thinking differently (Prensky, 2001b). Today's young learners are of a generation where the mouse and the keypad are as natural tools for interaction, communication and expression as the pen and the voice. The pervasive nature of ICT, the continual digital bombardment, has impacted upon every facet of life, and skills development in one area leads naturally into another. Being able to handle the on-screen games console helps the learner to drive and explore the virtual learning environment; navigating an entertainment DVD helps learners to use education-based video presentations. Learners today see images on screens as objects to be manipulated; they see scenes on the screen as environments to be explored and they recognise themselves as avatars, profiles and IDs. Ian Jukes' analysis speculates on the developments in our understanding of neuroscience, describes the concept of neuro-plasticity and asserts that intelligence is not fixed but develops as the capacity of neurons develop to make evermore complex structures, patterns and relations. Susan Greenfield, in her book *The Quest for Identity in the 21st Century*, drawing on evidence from neurological science, argues that the levels of visual stimulation when working, learning and being entertained today are impacting upon the brain and are reflected in terms of change in behaviour and personality (Greenfield, 2009).

Steven Johnson, in his book *Everything Bad Is Good for You* (Johnson, 2005), suggests that the challenges met by the digital generation when engaging with the television, computers and games has positive impacts upon the way they think. They are better able to make risk-taking judge-ments, they are well-motivated, they can deal with failure and they have developed thinking skills. The earlier TV generation experienced the singularity of plots and storylines that required no engagement by the viewer. The experiences of the current generation of television consumers are of complex scenarios, parallel plot lines, analogies and metaphors. Marc Prensky describes the younger generation as the digital natives – those learners brought up with the technologies and integrating their technology experiences fully with their traditional learning real world and kinaesthetic experiences.

Sustained and successful electronic game playing requires high levels of concentration, rapid eye–finger coordination, spatial awareness and memory of places, objects and sprites. It could be conjectured that there are transferable aspects to those skills that may support learning in more tradi-tional areas, as well as learning in computer-based environments. Usha Goswami believes that video gaming could be used to enhance skills of flexibility and behavioural inhibition. 'This would have a significant impact on their ability to regulate their own thoughts and behaviour, which is one of the developmental challenges of childhood and could be of great benefit to children' (Byron, 2008: 155).

Cognitive neuroscience research shows that an area of the brain called the frontal cortex plays a key role in self-regulation, in particular via inhibition. This brain region appears to govern the ability to inhibit particular actions in the light of new knowledge, and to shift attention flexibly as updating is required. (Goswami, 2008: 33)

Tanya Byron makes the assertion more strongly,

there are certain speculations we can make about the potential impact on children's development, including the possibility for them to lead to deeper learning, having a more significant impact on a child's sense of self and the potential for higher degrees of excessive use due to the 24/7 nature of the games. (Byron, 2008: 158)

A useful analysis of e-learning has arisen from Andrew Churches' interpretation of Bloom's cognitive taxonomy. The original hierarchy consists of, from lower order to higher order cognitive skills: knowledge, comprehension, application, analysis, synthesis and evaluation. More recently, it has been revised (Anderson and Krathwohl, 2001) and operationalised using the verbs: remembering, understanding, applying, analysing, evaluating and creating. Churches makes the observation that this analysis is not about the tools of online learning but it is about the learning. The analysis enables trainers and tutors to determine the nature of the learning and then look to the best tools to meet the needs of the learners (Churches, 2009). Steve Kennewell used the term 'affordances' of technology in a similar way, to identify what the technologies could do to support learning – what learning activities they supported – rather than considering the functionality of the software or online tools (Kennewell, 2001). Pat Maier and Adam Warren identified the values of learning technologies in terms of the learning that they supported (Maier and Warren, 2002).

For clarity, from this point onward, *e-learning* is only used to represent the psychology of learning when that learning is specifically dependent upon or arising from the impact of technology. E-learning is concerned with those learning patterns never witnessed before the introduction of technology. That is, e-learning is the actions of learners (pupils, students, trainees, tutees, etc.) to acquire curriculum-relevant skills, knowledge, understanding and attitudes through their use of technology-enabled teaching or technology-based resources. All other references to what is more generally called e-learning will be by use of specific terms described below.

In this section where the meaning of technology-enabled teaching and learning is being defined, it is important to realise that teaching and learning are not just about the technologies. The enablement also includes elements of:

- accessibility, user friendliness and social justice;
- personalisation, individualisation and learner–centeredness;
- open–learning and lifelong learning;
- bridging the digital divide within society, within families and between generations; and
- learner expectations.

- computer-assisted learning (CAL) or computer-based learning (CBL) or computer-assisted instruction (CAI) are usually used to describe practice that pre-dates the worldwide web;
- computer-assisted assessment (CAA), computer-based assessment (CBA), e-assessment, portfolio, e-portfolio (EP) all relate to the judgements of attainment and, occasionally, progress and mostly include feedback to the learner and teacher;
- virtual learning environment (VLE), managed learning environment (MLE), learning platform (LP), personalised learning environment (PLE), learner management system (LMS), content management system (CMS) all refer to various ways in which the teaching materials are managed or presented in a coherent, pedagogically structured way – characteristically protected by a username/password login where the learner is called/identified by their username with no control over their accessibility rights and representation;
- computer-mediated communication (CMC): e-mail, webmail, text (SMS) and media message service (MMS), picture messaging – the learner is identified by a telephone number or email address;
- social networking through internet messaging (IM), MSN Messenger, Twitter™, Facebook™, chat, chat rooms, where the learner is identified by a profile which they can modify;
- role-playing games (RPG), massively multiplayer online gaming (MMOG), massively multiplayer online role-playing games (MMORPG) utilised the virtual immersive environment (VIE) and 3D immersive applications (3Di), virtual worlds (VW) where the learner is represented by an avatar and can see themselves immersed in the learning environment;
- virtual reality (VR), augmented reality (AR);
- Web 2.0-related learning: web pages (HTML, HTPPS), wiki, web log (blog);
- computer-mediated conferencing (CMC): e-conferences, webcast, webinar, video conferencing (VC);
- media, presentations and publishing: pdf, CD, DVD, audio files, video files, MP3, jpeg, mov, Flash™, QuickTime™;
- technology-enabled learning: mobile learning (m-learning), web book, telephone, mobile phone, personal digital assistant (PDA), internet-enabled mobile phones (XDA), MP3 players, iPod™, podcasting, vodcasting.

Figure 1.2 The range and diversity of technology-enabled learning

A brief history of technology-enabled learning

In 1968, Herbert Hallworth in his review of the use of 'electronic computers' described a 'lop-sided development' within educational computing with the emphasis on programs to teach numeracy and little else. He describes the problem arising from a 'lack of personnel: it is difficult to find people with time and ability to use the equipment that already exists' and concludes that, in order to make an efficient use of computers, 'a prerequisite is the systematic training of both graduate and undergraduate students of education in computer techniques' (Hallworth, 1968: 240). The mid-1970s saw the arrival of the first microcomputers, including Apple™, IBM™, Commodore Business Machines™ and Atari™ (Atari, 2010), each making a contribution to the use of computers in the classroom. In 1975, the Commodore PET and, in 1977, the Apple II appeared in schools. They featured an integrated keyboard and tape device, sound and an input/output port. The software focussed on drill and practice computer-assisted instruction (CAI). In the UK, educational computing received a boost through the BBC Computer Literacy Project, Harold Wilson's 'white heat of technology' speech and the UK government's investment in computers for schools programmes based on two UK manufacturers, Acorn (Cambridge) and Research Machines (Oxford). Acorn, with its product the BBC Micro, eventually sold over a million computers to schools and homes. An early and celebrated use of computers is Seymour Papert's development of LOGO, a programming environment based on spatial awareness and list processing, in the 1960s (Papert, 1980; Abelson, 1982). Subsequently, programmable devices such as Bigtrak (Meredith and Briggs, 1982) and turtles appeared. In the UK, the Education Reform Act 1988 proposed a National Curriculum that included within the attainment targets for ten-year-olds (level 5),

Understand programs like
10 FOR NUMBER = 1 TO 10
20 PRINT NUMBER NUMBER
30 NEXT NUMBER. (Straker, 1989: 274)

Other computing activities for younger pupils included:

- give and understand instructions;
- help design a data collection sheet;
- use Logo commands;

- know that computers can be used for storing information (seven-year-olds);
- enter and access information in a simple database;
- create shapes using DRAW and MOVE commands;
- create a decision tree; and
- create, read and interpret a flow diagram.

The most able primary aged pupils were expected to 'know about two-state electronic devices and the application of such devices to logical decision making, binary counting and information storage' (Straker, 1989: 275). Sherry Turkle observed that people (children, parents and programmers) considered that the computer had a 'psychological' being with a sense of will and purpose (Turkle, 1984). It is something to which humans can 'relate'.

With the advent of English language-based programming languages like BASIC, computer literate teachers could develop lesson support materials. Small programs were written by teachers to meet specific learning objectives and particularly for students with special educational needs (Hope, 1986). Computer-assisted learning (CAL), promoted through a wide range of skills-orientated programs, dominated the scene in the early 1980s (Chandler, 1984; Govier, 1985). Then there was a rise in the importance of generic programs within the curriculum, including: handling information (databases), modelling (spreadsheets) and text manipulation (word processors) (Loveless, 1995; Scrimshaw, 1993; Squires and McDougall, 1994). The Grass database and Grasshopper spreadsheet, developed by Newman College, Birmingham under direct funding from the UK government, introduced pupils to the processes of handling information and communicating the results of searches, sorts and calculations. In the 1990s, the IT curriculum changed in response to the development of multimedia computers, videodiscs, media authoring tools and simulations. The windows-based computer interface also appeared. As a result of the change, more use was made of video and multimedia-enhanced teaching materials. Multimedia was used to create more interesting presentations of information (then known as interactive learning applications) and also as a tool for learners to create their own presentations (Acorn Computers, 1993; Heppell, 1993). These developments have not been without its critics because it has been seen as a move away from creative, engaging and challenging activities towards passive and undemanding information sources (Robertson, 1998).

The mid-1990s saw the arrival of the internet – e-mail and hypermail for communication, web browsing and web searching for handling information, satellite imagery and webcams for data capture, real time communications for modelling and exploring microworlds. Digital video, virtual reality, augmented reality and 3D systems further enriched the appearance of the teaching resources. By then, the computer was ubiquitous in US and UK classrooms. The late 1990s saw the rise of skills-based developments, such as the European Computer Driving Licence (ECDL, 2010) in the workplace, objective-based assessments in Key Stages 1 and 2 classrooms, such as those of the National Design and Technology Education Foundation (NDTEF), and elements of the UK New Opportunities (lottery) Funded (NOF) training for teachers. Both the NOF training and the initial teacher training programme emphasised understanding and application of ICT across the curriculum. There was a resurgence of computer managed learning under the guise of integrated learning systems (Wood, 1998; Williams, 2003) and open integrated learning systems replacing a lot of CAL driven activities.

At the turn of the millennium, the internet and, particularly, the world wide web began to dominate developments in educational technology and the popularity of CD ROM-based materials diminished. The single-version Encarta CD ROM could not compete with the ever-updating online encyclopaedias and new forms of information. In the UK, the National Grid for Learning and, later, the Secondary Strategy for ICT capability (DfES, 2002b) saw a renewed focus on computer suites in primary education and specialist teaching in secondary education (DfES, 2002a; Kennewell *et al.*, 2003) and investment in hardware (Cuban, 2001; Twining, 2002). Issues of teacher attitudes were at that time still factors in the effective use of ICT across the curriculum (Williams *et al.*, 1998; Amey, 2007) and in communication with students (Cunningham and Harris, 2003). More recently, we see the re-emergence of teaching ICT across the curriculum (ICTAC, pronounced *ick-tack*) in secondary schools (DfES, 2004a) and blended approaches (Condie and Livingston, 2007).

In 2003, the UK government released its policy outline for schools, colleges and universities *Progress towards a Unified E-Learning Strategy* consultation with the expectation that all UK schools can provide an online, transferable e-portfolio and access-from-home facility for all pupils and their parents (DfES, 2004b). This has driven the rush to virtual learning environments (VLEs) and other online facilities, such as pupil-authored websites, shared documents and email addresses for all pupils. There was a clearer understanding of the scope of technology-enabled learning emerging with a renewed interest in the principles of pedagogy (Conole *et al.*, 2004) and assessment (Bull and McKenna, 2004) in the form of computer-assisted assessment (CAA). The concept of cyber-spaces (virtual locations), colloquially known as 'the cloud', where learning can take place, is established.

The crossover between entertainment and education (edutainment) is increasing. The online gaming fraternity can lay claim to the educational value of many so-called gaming activities. The players exercise logic, exhibit good space perception and memory, strong control over their navigation (peregrination) and possess good eye–finger coordination. As a learning environment, the massively multiplayer online game (MMOG) environment can be considered a form of situated cognition, that allows 'learning to arise from active forms of engagement rather than the mere storage and retrieval of information from memory' (Young et al., 2006: 5). The year 2005 saw the release of the first 3D immersive environment designed specifically for young people – Teen Second Life® based on a similar grid and structure to the parent Second Life®, both developed by Linden Lab. Both use a free client program to access the in-world environment through an internet connection. The world is based on islands, owned by individuals and groups with most offering free access to the public. Second Life's popularity continues to grow, with 'more than 3000 servers and ... close to two million registered users' (Rymaszewski et al., 2008: iii). At the turn of the decade, teaching and learning through 3D immersive environments is now established as being suitable for all ages of learners.

In parallel with the development of virtual worlds requiring high internet bandwidth and large-screen desktop computers, there has been a move to make the opportunities for learning smaller and more mobile. Learning is taking place through text (SMS), media messaging (MMS), GPRS and, lately, 3G connected devices, web-books and XDAs (internet enabled personal digital assistants). This is broadening access to learning through increased flexibility, reduced costs and immediacy of the technology (Mohamad and Woollard, 2008; 2009; Shen et al., 2009).

Pedagogy, andragogy and cybergogy

The term 'pedagogy' is used to describe all forms of teaching strategies and principles of instruction in any learning environment and includes the activities of teachers, tutors and trainers.

Pedagogy is the heart of teaching. It is the rules and principles that guide effective and efficient activities that lead to learning. It is described equally as an art form and as a science. Paidagōgos is an ancient Greek word (παιδαγωγος.) meaning 'a slave who takes children to school to learn'. That idea is almost at odds with the current idea of pedagogy 'enabling learners to learn' but it does remind us that it is 'working with children and providing the opportunity to learn' and so the less rigorous meaning 'child-leading' is more appropriate to our current understanding of the process. Pedagogy is about teaching methods and principles of instruction. It is assisting students through interaction and activity in the ongoing academic and social events of the classroom. (Pritchard and Woollard, 2010: 45)

The term 'andragogy' is used when those teaching strategies and principles of instruction are focussed on adults and engaging adult learners with the structure of the learning experience. The term 'andragogy' (man-leading) was first used in 1833 by the German educator Alexander Kapp to describe the differences between working with adults and working with children. Malcolm Knowles developed the ideas into a theory of adult education. He felt that any experience that adults perceive as putting them in the position of being treated as children is bound to impact on their learning (Knowles, 1970). He described andragogy as 'the art and science of helping adults to learn' (Knowles, 1980: 43). A full description of andragogy is made in *Psychology for the Classroom: Constructivism and Social Learning* (Pritchard and Woollard, 2010: 45–50).

The term 'cybergogy' is used when those teaching strategies and principles of instruction are applied within a computer-based environment. Recent and important developments in our understanding of cybergogy have highlighted three aspects: the implications of moving about in a virtual world (or navigating in a 2D world); the difference in engagement of learners when immersed (Wang, 2007) in the activity; and the effects of experiencing learning through the medium of an avatar.

Two views of cybergogy are currently held; the first relates the principles of teaching to any form of technology-enabled learning, whereas the second focuses cybergogy towards the study of learning and application of teaching in a 3D immersive environment.

1 Cybergogy is used to describe the principles of teaching practice when those teaching strategies and methods of instruction are within any computer-based environment.
2 Cybergogy is used to describe the principles of teaching practice when those teaching strategies and methods of instruction are within a virtual world and engage the learner through the medium of an avatar.

In the first definition, cybergogy, like e-learning, has existed since the 1960s, although it has not been named as such until more recent times.

The application of educational technology has created a new teaching and learning concept – cybergogy. One of the central elements of cybergogy is the intent to combine fundamentals of both pedagogy and andragogy to arrive at a new approach to learning ... Cybergogy focuses on helping adults and young people to learn by facilitating and technologically enabling learner-centred autonomous and collaborative learning in a virtual environment. (Carrier and Moulds, 2003)

Central to the idea is that teaching through technology is not the same as face-to-face teaching. James Cronin and colleagues (Cronin *et al.*, 2009) argue that applications of cybergogy have characteristics in common with educational constructivism, namely, placing the learner at the centre of the teaching and learning experience. Their review of blended approaches in higher education is discussed in the next chapter.

The second definition is used by those who advocate that cybergogy applies only to the analysis of the principles of teaching practice in 3D immersive environments. Recent developments, emerging from computer-based game playing, that places the learner at the heart of and total focus of the computer display, in a way that no other learning technology has been able to achieve and the learning experience has become immersive. It is this new environment that is stimulating researchers (Kapp and O'Driscoll, 2010; Scopes, 2009) to understand a new way of teaching. They have defined the term 'cybergogy' as the 3D immersive teaching in virtual world environments.

Throughout this book, the principles of technology-enhanced learning will be called 'pedagogy'; if they are specifically directed to adults, then the term 'andragogy' is used. 'Cybergogy' is reserved for the teaching and learning approaches that place the learner in the focal point of the activity, when it is through 3D immersive environments with avatars. As with pedagogy, there are many principles of practice of cybergogy but, unlike the thousands of years of history celebrated by pedagogy, cybergogy history is measured in single years. Consequently, many aspects of technology-enabled teaching will be described in terms of traditional pedagogy as well as the emerging models and terminology of cybergogy.

Mapping the psychology

The developments in technology-enabled teaching and learning have occurred quickly in its short life from the early microprocessors through to today's sophisticated application of web-based and mobile technologies.

The previous sections outlined the pervasive and impactful influence that technology is having upon classroom, lecture theatre, training centre and learner practice. The classroom is changing, and so are the learners. Prensky (2001a) coined the phrase 'digital natives' for those learners spending their formative years in the online world; they are 'used to receiving information really fast', 'prefer random access' and 'thrive on instant gratification and frequent rewards'. The others, the digital immigrants, may struggle to work as efficiently in such an environment or struggle to understand this new way of thinking and being and so not utilise the technologies to the best effect. John Cuthell, when discussing the autonomous learner, draws similar conclusions in his book *Virtual Learning* (Cuthell, 2002).

- A significant number of students expect to do more work at home than in school.
- Many students regard knowledge of 'how to' as more important than 'what'.
- The students' personal computers are the vehicles for learning.
- The students' patterns of learning are not found in the classroom.
- The computer accommodates the range of intelligences (Gardner, 1983) and preferred means of learning, impacting on students' attainment.

Source: Based on Cuthell (2002: 149–150).

Figure 1.3 The changing face of learning

This next section considers the interaction between the learners, teaching and the psychology of the classroom and maps each in relation to the developing practices.

There are three major underpinning approaches to learning theory, simply described as behaviourist, cognitivist and constructivist. There is an increased complexity when we consider the different aspects of each area of learning theory, the proliferation of approaches that connect an aspect of theory with a specific teaching approach and the overlap and combination of theories as they become formalised in pedagogic practice. Figure 1.4 describes some of the relationships between the major areas of learning theory and the different and diverse areas of technology-enabled teaching and learning. To guide the design of the evaluation process with regard to pedagogy, a model relating learning theory to design is proposed.

- Behaviourism gives us: a focus on skills and observable evidence of learning; task analysis and structured learning opportunities; changing attitudes and responses; and objective assessment of progress.
- Cognitivism gives us a consideration of: different ways of learning;

different types of learning; developing stages of learning; intelligence, learning styles and various strategies for learning.

■ Social constructivism gives us: engaged learning through activity and communication; collaboration and cooperative activities to support learning; communities of practice; and socially constructed ideas and understanding.

Other theories reflecting psychological constructs and technology-enabled learning are: motivation (Bolliger *et al.*, 2010; Garris *et al.*, 2002; Keller, 1999; Maslow, 1943; Prensky, 2001a); maturity (Erikson, 1968; Salmon, 2000); beliefs (Askew *et al.*, 1997; Dwyer *et al.*, 1990; Medwell *et al.*, 2001; Turner-Bisset, 2001; Yero, 2002), culture (Michael, 2000) and the regulation of learning (Perrenoud, 1998; Zimmerman and Schunk, 2011).

Major learning theories in relation to technology-enabled teaching

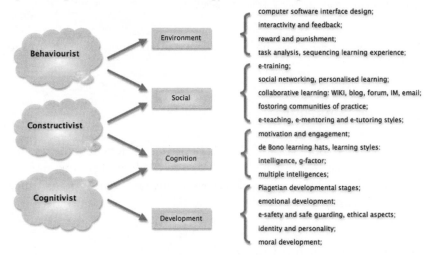

Figure 1.4 Mapping the psychology of e-learning

To help identify the psychological aspects of new technologies, the next model (Figure 1.5) identifies the affordances in terms of change that the online learning strategies enable. The model identifies the six major aspects of learning derived from theories and serves as a useful conceptual framework when considering the impact of new technologies on learning. Each aspect has associated with it a number of key questions to ask of the resource (application, artefact or system) when considering the design, development, implementation and evaluation.

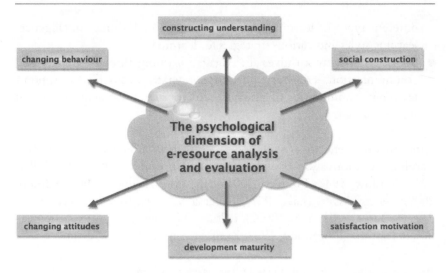

Figure 1.5 Analysing the psychological dimension of e-resources

The following questions help elucidate the meaning of each area of analysis.

Changing behaviour

How does the resource identify learning outcomes? How does the resource reward/reinforce appropriate/good responses? How does the resource celebrate success? Does it provide clear information, advice and guidance? Is it structured?

Constructing understanding

How does the resource prescribe learning activities? How does the resource enable structured experiences? How does the resource enable the presentation of ideas? How does the resource build upon current knowledge and understanding?

Socially engaged learning

How does the resource foster cooperation? How does the resource foster collaboration? How does the resource support communication? How does the resource sustain the learners' engagement in the process? How does the resource foster communities of practice?

Satisfaction and motivation

How does the resource appeal to the learners' aesthetic and personal desires? How does the resource meet the learners' expectations? How does the resource meet the personalisation agenda (student-centeredness, individualisation)? How does the resource meet the needs relating to age, gender (GLBT&H), ethnicity, culture, faith and belief? How does the resource meet the needs of different learning styles? How does the resource meet basic human needs?

Development and maturity

How does the resource respond differently to the different stages of development of the learners? How does it meet the needs arising from the stage of cognitive development? Does it reflect age and social appropriateness in the materials?

Changing attitudes

How does the resource impact upon attitudes? How does the resource promote particular value sets? How does the resource enable exploration of values, faiths and beliefs? Does it provide clear ethical instruction? Does it provide clear moral guidance and example?

Summary

E-learning is a special kind of learning that only occurs by means of technology and is associated with the newly acquired abilities of the digital natives. Technology-enabled teaching is the pervasive use of technology to support teaching and learning in all fields of teaching, training and tutoring with all ages and abilities of learners, from infants through to silver surfers, those with special educational needs and those with high-level academic and learning skills.

The history of computers in education informs current practice and the understanding of why and how technology can support learning. The different aspects of technology-enabled learning reflect the different and contrasting theories of learning, with some aspects being underpinned by behaviourist theory, others by social constructivism and some by cognitivist approaches.

Activities

- Consider, in the light of the content of this chapter, the major differences between the earlier activities of computers in schools and the more recent descriptions of technology-enabled learning.
- Consider the personalisation, socialisation, emotional and motivational aspects of technology-enabled learning and how they relate to your current practice.
- Consider the evidence for a change in capability of digital natives and their capacity to utilise and benefit from the pervasive use of technology in their education.

2

Research

By the end of the chapter you will be able to:

- identify different approaches to research and their contribution to evaluating the use of technology in teaching and learning;
- identify the values of meta-analysis and critique and how the conclusions of individual research projects might be better judged;
- appreciate the contribution of technology-enabled teaching to social learning (Bandura, 1977); and
- identify the key issues of e-safety that relate to the learners for whom you are responsible.

Technology-enabled teaching and learning have been under considerable scrutiny from the academic educational fraternity and much is written in celebration of initiatives, exemplification of the affordances and the examination of learning. Identifying, through rigorous research methods, the efficacy or efficiency of e-learning methods is not easy. As David Mitchell observes, the paradigm for most empirical educational research is based on 'an input-process-output model which assumes causality from independent to dependent variable' (Mitchell, 1997: 53). The approach requires a high level of mathematical rigour both in establishing the quality of the raw data and in the application of statistics, such as t-test, correlations, analysis of variance, etc. He also identifies the problems associated with 'passing subjective judgements off as measurements ... by attaching numbers to constructs for which none of the properties of measurable magnitude are met' (1997: 53). With that caution in mind, this chapter begins with the description of a meta-analysis of the research carried out between 1996 and 2008. The other sections deal with particular foci of research: the collaborative and social aspects of technology-enabled learning, the classroom settings for e-learning and the technology focus of research. Finally, there is a description of a critique of one important aspect of learning through technology – e-safety.

Online learning: a meta-analysis of research

Meta-analysis and systematic review of experimental results and literature constitute an important research methodological approach. The result is more powerful than the sum of the parts because the method exposes trends and patterns that are not identifiable through scrutiny of the individual sources of evidence in isolation. Bias is avoided by obtaining as much material/data as possible; but the collection of that material must meet the strict selection criteria. Meta-analysis provides strong evidence because it avoids misrepresentation of the evidence. The quality of all the individual items in a review is judged against strict criteria that are set down before the review begins. The explicit nature of the criteria associated with the approach means that the process is open to scrutiny and could be replicated; checks can be made by independent parties after the review has been published. Importantly, because the protocol is set down before the review starts, the results cannot influence the procedures; that is, a particularly strong piece of evidence cannot change the focus of the study. As described in the advice from the Evidence for Policy and Practice Information and Co-ordinating Centre (EPPI) at the Institute of Education, London,

> any good research, the methods for a systematic review are made explicit in a 'protocol' before it starts. This helps to reduce bias in the review process, for example by ensuring that reviewers' procedures are not overly influenced by the results of studies they find. If changes are needed to the protocol as the review progresses these need to be noted in the review's final report and the rationale for making changes made clear. (EPPI, 2010)

A meta-analysis of the results of many investigations enables an overall picture to be established. The degree of importance (the effect size) of an individual study can be estimated as the difference between the mean for that study and the mean for the control group of that study divided by the standard deviation of the combined results.

In 2009, the United States Department of Education commissioned a systematic study of the literature regarding practices in online learning (US

DoE, 2009). This study considers the research literature from 1996 through July 2008 and identifies more than a thousand empirical studies of online learning. The systematic nature of the study requires the researchers to specify the type of resources that will be searched, the selection criteria, the criteria for analysis and quality assessment and the procedure for weighting and presenting individual works. The study provides four important areas of information. First, it identifies a conceptual framework for online learning that relates directly to the psychology of learning; it establishes what is and what is not online learning. Second, it establishes a quantitative means of calculating the relative effect of introducing online learning, called the 'effect size'; only papers that present sufficient information for that to be calculated are included in the analysis. Third, it provides a rich source of reliable studies that illustrate ways in which innovative practice can be developed. Finally, and most importantly, it provides a bottom-line statement as to the value of technology-supported teaching.

This conceptual framework for online learning helps to guide the literature search and review. The US study's definition of online learning has three considerations:

- Does it replace face-to-face teaching or enhance face-to-face teaching (known as 'blended learning')?
- What type of underlying pedagogy determines the learning experience?
- Is the activity synchronous or asynchronous?

The classroom psychology questions relate to both the means of learning and the motivation. The study identifies three forms of learning experience:

- expository, didactic instruction where the technology delivers the knowledge;
- active learning which engages the learner in exercises, quizzes, mind-tools, etc.; and
- interactive learning involving collaboration and peer-to-peer or peer-to-teacher communication.

The belief of teachers is that 'the way in which teaching takes place impacts upon the quality of learning' and some teachers believe that 'the quality of learning is proportional to the level of interactivity'.

The concept of synchronicity is important – are activities asynchronous or synchronous? The Carroll diagram in Table 2.1 represents the main online learning devices and identifies whether they are predominantly used by learners at the same time or at different times, as and when they wish.

Table 2.1 Synchronous and asynchronous online learning opportunities

	Synchronous	Asynchronous
Communication (two-way)	chat chat rooms internet messenger virtual worlds	email Web 2.0 forum
Information	e-conferences webinar (web conferences) video conferencing	web pages wiki podcasting RSS
Recording	chat history electronic footprint VLE statistics	blog Twitter™ Facebook™

The e-learning facilities are represented as a dichotomy but in reality there are degrees of difference. For example, people can sustain a synchronous exchange of ideas through email by being continually logged on and replying immediately. Conversely, instant messenger becomes an asynchronous device when a correspondent leaves a message if the recipient is logged off. The value of synchronous exchange over asynchronous devices is not clear-cut; studies generally yield no significant differences (Gunawardena and McIsaac, 2004). In fact, such debate misses the point that, as with all forms of technology, it is the nature of the learning aims or the learner's preferred mode of learning that should determine the technology and method of employment. However, in this debate, Stefan Hrastinski raises an interesting point regarding the relationship between the asynchronous/synchronous nature of technology and the psychology of learning, whether it is cognitive or personal (social) in nature. He asserts that 'personal participation describes a more arousing type of participation appropriate for less complex information exchanges, including the planning of tasks and social support. Cognitive participation describes a more reflective type of participation appropriate for discussions of complex issues'. He suggests that 'other things being equal, synchronous e-learning better supports personal participation and asynchronous e-learning better supports cognitive participation' (Hrastinski, 2008: 5). As described in Figure 2.1 there are many routes and forms of communication in the classroom and in technology-enabled learning. An important factor that influences the effectiveness of the learning process is the interaction that exists between the teacher and the learner. The work of Baruch Offir and colleagues suggests that different interactions have different effects and they have investigated the differences between asynchronous and synchronous. They conclude, observations and interviews which we held with the students helped clarify the information that was obtained using the quantitative research tools, and showed that the presence of a teacher–student interaction which accompanies the learning process is very important for all learners. However, students with high-level thinking can overcome the low-level of interactions in asynchronous learning ... the interaction level between the students and the teacher and among the students was found to be a significant factor in determining the effectiveness of the teaching method. (Offir *et al.*, 2008: 1172)

Figure 2.1 shows the relationship between asynchronous and synchronous approaches and the nature of learning.

cognitive and social natures of learning	
cognitive engagement	**social engagement**
email (1:1)	chat (1:1)
email (1:many)	blog (many:1)
forum WIKI (many:many)	chat room (many:many)
long – degree of separation between comment and response	short – degree of separation between comment and response
understanding expressing concluding	planning collaborating cooperating
cognitivist constructivist constructionist	social constructivist
asynchronous engagement	**synchronous engagement**
asynchronous and synchronous nature of technology	

Figure 2.1 The cognitive/social asynchronous/synchronous dimensions of learning

The figure illustrates the parallelism between synchronicity and the nature of learning. It also illustrates that the communication, regardless of synchronicity, can be one-to-one or many-to-many in nature. The intensity of the communication has an implication for social constructivism. There is also an implication for the preferred learning style of the individual and for physical/social needs of the individual.

This US meta-analysis of e-learning draws the following conclusions:

- The 'effect sizes were larger for studies that compared blended learning conditions with face-to-face instruction than for studies that compared purely online learning with face-to-face instruction' (US DoE, 2009: 38).
- *'The majority of...* studies that directly compared purely online and blended learning conditions found no significant differences in student learning' (US DoE, 2009: 38).
- *'Seven of the eight studies found no significant differences'* when using media such as embedded video and graphics (US DoE, 2009: 40). The analysis suggests that the inclusion of media is not necessarily an efficient mechanism for enhancing learning. The video is acting as a medium for knowledge and nothing else. The study cites the work of Zhang *et al.* (2006), which suggests that it is the interactive nature of the use of video that is key to its value in supporting learning.
- With regard to the important consideration of learning experience (described above as expository, active and interactive) the study found the results mixed 'with respect to the relative effectiveness of the three learning experience types' (US DoE, 2009: 41). It suggests that there is an advantage to giving learners a degree of control over their learning experience.

The main finding arising from this study is that there is little rigorous, quantitative research enabling the effect of online working to be measured. The study does conclude that, 'students who took all or part of their class online performed better, on average, than those taking the same course through traditional face-to-face instruction' (US DoE, 2009: xiv). However, the study warns that other factors may influence the better student performance, such as time spent on the tasks.

Collaborative and social learning

Computer-supported collaborative learning (CSCL) has been established as an affordance of ICT in teaching and learning since the early 1990s, with international conferences celebrating the work of researchers, practitioners and learners in 1995, 1997 and 2001 (ITCOLE, 2003). Recent research (Lockhorst *et al.*, 2010) further explores the affordances of CSCL, focusing on the training of teachers where the teachers in training were given compulsory collaborative tasks. Those tasks included a range of 'products' and different assessment methods including group, shared, blended, port-folio and reflective strategies.

Shared debate proposition on future history teaching assessed by face-to-face discussion of group propositions and reflections on group work in student portfolio.

A group list of criteria for effective teaching methods assessed by face-to-face discussion of group propositions and reflections on group work in student portfolio.

A series of lessons plans assessed by face-to-face group presentation and reflections on group work in student portfolio.

Description and comparison of educational curricula assessed by face-to-face group presentation and reflections on group work in student portfolio.

Design, revision and performance of a lesson assessed by peer feedback and student portfolio.

Small-group research assessed by face-to-face presentation and collective report.

Collection of information on 'teaching outside the classroom' assessed through a collective face-to-face presentation.

Reflection on teaching performance assessed through a written group story including reflections on teaching practice.

Figure 2.2 Examples of activities enhanced by computer-supported collaboration

'The results indicate that reflection-oriented tasks stimulated participation, and in combination with task structure also interaction. Structured tasks which required critical reflection on personal experiences and perspectives triggered task-related communication and a deep level of information exchange' (Lockhorst *et al.*, 2010: 63). The interesting findings arising from this work come through the analysis of both the qualitative and quantitative data based on three perspectives:

1 participation (the frequency of joining in and contributing);
2 interaction (sustained response to other contributions and the nature of the threads); and
3 the nature of communication.

The final perspective was further measured by considering the level of information exchange (task-related responses) and the nature of their regu-latory communication, including responses related to planning, organisa-tion of tasks, technical issues and evaluative responses, where the contributors are determining the skills and knowledge of group members or expressing feelings and thoughts.

This work brings a better understanding of two important concepts of online communication: threads and depth of contribution.

> A thread is a continuous, but perhaps diverging, collection of contributions (sometimes called posts) on a particular topic under a specified name (subject) usually started by an opening statement or question, displayed in chronological order. It is a continuous train of thought contributed to by different people and, therefore, it is at the heart of the social constructivist view of knowledge exchange and reaching an agreed understanding.

The thread can be developed synchronously, as in chat, chat room, conferencing and webinar discussions, or asynchronously, as in blogs, wiki, email exchanges and shared documents. Synchronicity becomes blurred in some instances when, say, people are exchanging emails simultaneously (and perhaps should be using a better online tool such as chat) or they are simultaneously editing the same online document. Chronology sometimes becomes blurred, particularly in the case of wikis and shared documents, where the display is of the latest version and the chronological order of contributions is recorded elsewhere. The developing nature of the thread and the degree to which contributors make reference to previous texts is a measure of their depth. Figure 2.3 describes the generic aspects of a forum-type thread.

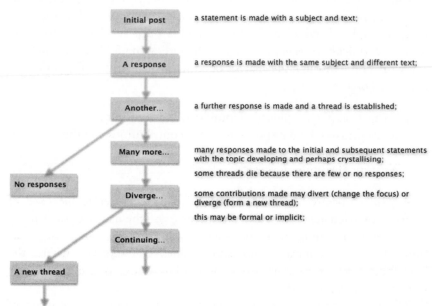

Figure 2.3 The life of a thread – key points in the chronology

The depth of a thread can be measured in a variety of ways according to purpose. The following analysis indicates those areas of concern when the contributors are learners and the act of learning is of paramount importance. Table 2.2 identifies the key parameters.

The strong conclusions drawn from the work of Ditte Lockhorst and colleagues (Lockhorst *et al.*, 2010: 75) indicate that collaborative activities by teachers play an important role in their initial training and their continuing professional development, and that technology enhances that process.

Table 2.2 Measuring engagement in threaded discussions – the degree of social construction

Response rate	The number of responses or posts is a crude measure of popularity, surface engagement or participation with the thread; it does not take into account the level of lurking or non-participatory views and may therefore not fully estimate the potential learning taking place.
View rate	The number of views or visits is another crude measure but reveals attention to the topic under consideration and might indicate that steps need to be taken to ensure full engagement in the discourse.
Interaction	This measure requires discourse analysis to determine if responses are reflecting the previous contributions and building upon the body of knowledge or mutual understanding. Less good interaction is when responses do not make connections with the content of previous messages.
Surface or deep	Individual contributions can be surface or deep. 'Surface-level communication refers to routine learning activities, without much engagement and reflection, with much memorisation, and problem solving with just a limited conceptual understanding. Deep-level communication refers to learning activities that are focused on understanding, conceptual analysis, use of previous knowledge and experiences, and argumentations' (Lockhorst *et al.*, 2010: 68).
Evaluative (deep)	Evaluative communication contains elements of reflection; that reflection may refer to the self (feelings and thoughts) connected to the focus of the thread or the reflection may refer to other people or other things, for example, 'assessment of the tasks or appraisal of knowledge and skills of group members' (Lockhorst *et al.*, 2010: 68). Being a reflective practitioner is seen to be an important feature of a successful teacher (Brindley, 2002; Turner-Bisset, 2001).
Functional	Much of the exchange observed does not relate to the development of knowledge and an agreed understanding. Contributions focus upon the functional nature of the task. 'Planning refers to communication in which the performance of learning activities is set out. Organisational includes division of labour, tasks, and tools' (Lockhorst *et al.*, 2010: 68). A surface-level aspect of functional exchanges relates to responses about technical issues.
Phatic (surface)	Surface-level communication is associated with the social exchanges or phatic expressions (Malinowski, 1923).

Their research shows that the design of the tasks has an important influence upon the outcomes. Their conclusions identify a number of features that influence the degree of interaction and communication within a group and the participation in online tasks. First, tasks that require a single group product are more effectively developed if the product is to be used afterwards by the individuals of that group. The activities that have strong structures with a degree of didacticism can compensate for low learner participation but participation can be encouraged through the requirement to be reflective and to give peer feedback. Participation is also encouraged by reflection and peer feedback, which also promote learner communication. Complex tasks with defined roles for participants, choices of outcomes and controversial or unusual propositions promote communication. Discussion-focussed tasks and tasks relating to personal perspectives promote communication.

The term 'engagement' covers both participation in the task (thinking and doing) and communication between peers. It is at the heart of Vygotsky's dynamic involvement between the learner and the social context. That is, knowledge is a social product, and learning is a social process. The social constructivist view is that meaning and understanding are forged out of an agreement between social partners. The following key prompts enumerated in Figure 2.4 identify the way in which online tasks should be designed to promote that social and cognitive engagement – participation and communication.

Products of tasks should be usable and/or be required to be used;

instructions should be clear and expectations explicit;

collaboration should be required;

cooperation should be expected;

peer review and peer assessment should be integrated;

choice should be enabled but delimited; and

prompts should be interesting (unusual, perhaps controversial).

Source: Based on Lockhorst *et al.* (2010).

Figure 2.4 Promoting participation and interaction

James Cronin and colleagues (Cronin *et al.*, 2009) report a case study based on an online discussion forum used to help teach a diploma in European Art History. Their conclusions are interpreted in a constructivist paradigm emphasising the role of collaboration, blended approaches and structured learning experiences (learning enactments). The role of e-moderation is identified as being key to the social constructivist processes of step-by-step concept 'formation, refinement, application, and revision … [that is] fully visible to student peers as well as their mentors' (Cronin *et al.*, 2009: 209) supporting the idea that interactive and socially engaging activities, such as forums, blogs, journals and chat rooms, are appropriate strategies for enabling learners to develop their understanding. That is social constructivism in action. Important aspects of the actions include: clarifying concepts, making propositions and establishing meaningful links and relationships. Good methods for structuring knowledge should result in simplifying concepts, generating new propositions and increasing the manipulation of information. Jerome Bruner (1966) identified that these are the skills of teachers that enable learning to take place and they are now seen as the affordances of online systems that similarly enable learning.

James Cronin's work was developed through a commercial virtual learning environment (VLE) (Blackboard™) and used Gilly Salmon's five-stage model (Salmon, 2000: 115–119) to ensure the online experience catered for all levels of expertise in online communication and also to inform the forum design. (See Chapter 3 for an outline of the theory.) The aim of the forum on the VLE was to increase the contact time that the learners had with the materials and with each other. 'It was anticipated that the discussion board would support and enhance discussion beyond face-to-face tutorial contact' (Cronin *et al.*, 2009: 210). Through the context of the Art History course the researchers are able to interpret what Meyer and Land (2003; 2006) call a 'threshold concept' which 'represents a transformed way of understanding, or interpreting, or viewing something, which must be understood before a learner can progress' (Cronin *et al.*, 2009: 211). That the transformation may be sudden or protracted over a considerable period of time. By identifying the difficult concepts in art history, such as students' understanding of the social and political context of the work, there is a better comprehension of how the forum can aid in grasping difficult concepts. An interesting statistic arising from the work of Cronin and colleagues is that, although the forum received in the region of 900 views for each module (by about 70 per cent of the students), there were far fewer posts, ranging from 21 to 40 in different modules (by about one third of the students). The online public (http://www.urbandiction ary.com/define.php?term=lurker, Wikipedia) and researchers (Nonnecke and Preece, 2000; Richards, 2003; 2009) identify the non-participants as 'lurkers' and, according to this research, lack of confidence accounts for this online silence. The students who show more frequent participation are the higher achievers in the group.

The researchers obtained the views of the participants through face-to-face discussion (focus group) centring on deep learning, support, barriers and improvements associated with the VLE and its resources. The conclusions include that:

- the VLE would be more valuable if introduced at the start of the programme;
- the VLE was valuable in promoting better understanding and knowledge;
- the VLE supported learning by providing the resources;
- the developing resources of the lecturer's notes were particularly valued;
- 'initial feelings of inadequacy, lack of self-confidence, constraints of time and issues of user-friendliness in site navigation were factors contributing to online silence';
- 'feelings of intimidation or embarrassment' and 'a sense of reticence' impeded participation;
- factors of 'user-friendliness' were cited as impedances with the structure of forum and sub-forum not helping ease of access;
- 'being named' and associated directly with the contribution was seen as a significant impediment to participation (Cronin *et al.*, 2009).

Reflecting on this research, we can identify themes that reappear in Chapter 3 when the concepts of the digital immigrant and digital native are explored as well as the construct of digital divide and disenfranchisement. James Cronin relates some of these issues to the concept of Pierre Bourdieu's knowledge capital and explanation of inequalities in educational achievement.

Using ICT to support teaching

The classroom use of ICT is an important aspect of technology-enhanced teaching. It is a rich mix of technologies, both hardware and software, being local, across the school network and across the internet, and being synchronous with the classroom teaching and asynchronous, supporting out-of-classroom learning. Consequently, methods of teaching and the ways of learning are equally complex and diverse.

The research, ImpaCT2, conducted between 2000 and 2002, is an intense analysis of classroom practice incorporating ICT and exposes the models of working, the technology in use and the means of learning to scrutiny and evaluation (DfES, 2002a). The contributors, drawn from four leading universities in the UK, each have made subsequent contributions to our understanding of the role of ICT in learning. The results clearly define the potential of ICT to enhance learning. An important feature is that the measures are drawn from information provided by the pupils and their experiences of using ICT.

The research identifies the areas where the use of ICT is having an impact upon outcomes – that is, the grades pupils achieve in assessments. In every case of 'lower use of ICT', there is no significant change in outcomes. An immediate conclusion must be drawn that, either ICT is used fully and in an integrated way, or there is little point in using it as a teaching strategy. Many argue that the use of ICT is of value in itself for preparing pupils for life, work and leisure. In a world where ICT has a pervasive presence, then some use of ICT which does not have an impact on standards in other subjects can be justified. The report shows that where there is a high use of ICT, then there are statistically significant gains in learners' examination results and scores in standardised tests.

The research results for Key Stage 4 (14- to 16-year-olds) dramatically illustrate the difference in gains in some subjects between those pupils exposed to low use of ICT and those exposed to high use. 'The differences are slight and not statistically significant for English, mathematics and history. The differences in performance are much more considerable for science ... The greatest difference ... is found in modern foreign languages' (DfES, 2002a: 31) The increased performances in design technology were significant in all cases.

The features of the ICT usage that provided such gains in science were:

■ localised hardware resources – computer-based subject teaching areas;
■ the use of the internet for revision and research where topics require up-to-date information;
■ the use of simulations (enabling metaphor, analogy, modelling of the cognitivist school); and
■ using ICT to provide instant feedback on strengths and weaknesses.

These observations can be interpreted, using the language of the major learning theories, as:

■ context-based learning;
■ exploring material to construct own understanding (internet and simulations); and
■ positive reinforcement of appropriate/correct responses (feedback).

The localised resources enable better contextualised learning opportunities. The use of the internet and simulations enable constructivist approaches to knowledge acquisition and development of understanding. The instant feedback supports behaviourist positive reinforcement and encouragement.

In other subject areas of Key Stage 4, the positive effects of using presentation technologies, such as digital projectors and interactive whiteboards, were noted. These provide immediate feedback, interactivity and the potential for the teacher to celebrate achievement and reinforce positive contributions to class work. In geography, the use of data handling and graphing packages was noted; again, these applications enable learners to explore the materials, ask 'what if' questions, make hypotheses and test them, thus giving a high level of engagement with the subject.

Comparable results arose from the ImpaCT2 research for Key Stages 1, 2 and 3, but with different subjects responding differently.

> There is no consistent relationship between the average amount of ICT use reported for any subject at a given key stage and its apparent effectiveness in raising standards. It therefore seems likely that the type of use is all important. (DfES, 2002a: 3)
>
> Early impact studies demonstrated that young people's use of technology to support learning across the curriculum could have significant positive impacts in a range of subjects. The embedding of technology across whole schools emerged as a key factor in improving outcomes. (Becta, 2010)

At a similar time to the ImpaCT2 studies, another research programme, originally based around Manchester but extending across the whole of the UK, investigated ICT practice, proposed a structuring of ICT teaching and evaluated the results. Bridget Somekh and Matthew Pearson led the Pedagogies with E-learning Resources (PELRS) action research project (Somekh and Pearson, 2002) with the research question 'Could we organise teaching and learning in radically different ways now we have the internet, internet-look-alike CD/DVD materials, digital imaging, video and other new technologies?'

The project was characterised by the fact that teachers were fully involved in the development, data gathering and reporting processes. It was the teachers' professional skills and knowledge that contributed to the design and implementation of the pedagogy. PELRS was also committed to working with pupil-researchers. The empirical data was gathered through observation, teacher reflections, pupils' work, digital videoing and photographs. The pupil-researchers were involved in the interpretation of the videos and provided valuable insights into the processes of the project, including motivation, excitement and enthusiasm. The first priority of the

PELRS project was to create transformative learning experiences for pupils in the participating schools, including both the pupil-researchers and their peers.

The proposed generic pedagogic framework places the learning focus (devised by teachers and pupils) at the centre of:

- the pupils in their context of family and peers;
- the teachers and other adults who influence learning;
- the location of the ICT, whether it is school or home (hardware) or virtual.

The first point is well made by publications from Futurelab and GoodPlay. The report *Developing the Home–School Relationship Using Digital Technologies* (Futurelab, 2010) concludes that the learning process is not one that is isolated within the school but children need to make connections between what they learn and their life experiences and the children need to be the mediators between the family context for learning and the school. Schools should not be imposing or transplanting school practices of teaching and learning into the home environment. That is 'unlikely to fit easily with parent's skills and the cultures of home ... valuing and developing home practices may be more successful' (Futurelab, 2010: 59). The value of impartial advice and support for parents as they adjust to and accept practices, similar to those that have been criticised in the recent past (such as, online games, 3D graphics, social networking, widespread use of the open internet) cannot be overstated. The GoodPlay Project based at Stanford University recognises the issues of the different perceptions of children and parents and provides a very useful guide (GoodPlay Project, 2009).

The PELRS conclusions are described as 'transformative learning outcomes':

1 creative learning
2 active citizenship
3 cognitive engagement
4 meta-cognition (Somekh and Pearson, 2006: 4).

This work has implications for the psychological aspects of technology-enabled learning:

- creative learning is social construction;
- changing behaviour is reflected in active citizenship;
- cognitive engagement is about constructing understanding; and

■ meta-cognition relates to the developing mind and understanding the nature of learning.

More recent research identifies other technology-related factors that are impacting upon educational attainments. From a longitudinal study of people in England carried out by the Institute for Fiscal Studies, one factor identified is the level of material resources, such as computer and internet access in the home. They 'are important in explaining the gap in educational attainment between young people from rich and poor backgrounds' (Chowdry et al, 2009: 8). However, the PERLS report, in contrast to the school-focussed, curriculum-focussed ImpaCT reports (DfES, 2002a), links educational gain most strongly with the motivation and attitudes of the pupil.

Technology-mediated learning

Podcasts are audio files, usually in the form of MP3 files, that can be played through a computer, a website/web page, a mobile telephone or an MP3 player. The medium for storage is, conveniently, a memory stick, memory card or the hard drives of computers. Podcasting is the distribution of those files, usually by subscription on a website, after which the files are sent automatically to the computer (Kelly, 2005; Patterson, 2006; Rogan et al., 2005). The term is a portmanteau of 'iPod,' and 'broadcast' (Patterson, 2006). Podcasting enables the user to have fresh content downloaded to their computer or iPod on demand or by schedule (Harden, 2006). This process can be described as the first application based on real simple synchronisation (RSS) to capture the imagination of users and developers of online audio media (Curran et al., 2006). With Apple's introduction of its video iPod, podcasting has moved into the video arena too. Instead of creating MP3 files, video podcasting uses the next generation of MPEG file format called MP4 (Patterson, 2006). Podcasting with video content is called 'vodcasting'.

An important feature of podcasts is the ease of access; they are simple to download onto computers, laptops, internet-enabled mobile phones and can subsequently be transferred to MP3 players for more flexibility of use (Fose and Mehl, 2007). For the learner they have an advantage over traditional online training because of the possibility of multitasking; it is possible to listen to a podcast whilst doing other non-audio tasks, such as driving a car, relaxing with eyes closed or mowing the lawn. Podcasts can carry the human voice, which can convey conviction, compassion, empathy, experience, ethnicity and gender (Donnelly and Berge, 2006; Harden, 2006). Recent research (Bolliger et al., 2010) into the efficacy of using podcasts in teaching and learning has established a rationale for their use.

The report 'Impact of podcasting on student motivation in the online learning environment' (Bolliger et al., 2010) details the investigation of podcasts being used with nearly 200 students across 14 online courses focussing on students' attention, confidence, satisfaction and appreciation of the relevance of the resource. This relates to the psychology model (Chapter 1) that recognises the importance of motivation (satisfaction and perceived relevance) and attitudes (confidence). The focus of the research on motivation gives rise to key questions about the use of any technology with teaching and learning. The Instructional Materials Motivation Survey (IMMS) (Keller, 1979; 1999) is a device for measuring the motivational impact of a teaching strategy – the four key aspects of John Keller's analysis are attention, relevance, confidence and satisfaction (ARCS). Attention is the degree to which the learner engages with the material, either because of the sensory arousal (vivid colours, audio, movement, etc.) or the cognitive engagement (inquiry arousal) of the learner. The relevance of the learning activity has an impact upon the motivation – John Keller proposes several strategies: suggesting to the learner how the experience will build upon their current knowledge, skills and understanding parallel with the Zone of Proximal Development (Vygotsky, 1962; 1978); making the activity of immediate value and valuable in the future (providing positive reinforcement for any learning); matching the activity with the learner's perceived needs; modelling the desired outcomes and giving choice or options. The degree to which the learning experience increases motivation is dependent upon the confidence that is instilled in the learner. Key aspects that support that situation include: clear learning outcomes expressed in learner-speak; performance criteria that are SMART (specific, measurable, achievable, reinforceable and timely); experiencing success; success being notified, acknowledged and celebrated; and learner control through choice. The learning process must be rewarding in order to establish a sense of satisfaction. The rewards can be intrinsic (pride, joy, well-being, sense of achievement, etc.) or extrinsic (awards, certificates, praise, acknowledgement, etc.).

The Doris Bolliger research gathered students' responses relating to the four areas of attention, relevance, confidence and satisfaction (Figure 2.5). The qualitative analysis arising from the data indicated that podcasts assisted many learners by helping them to understand the instructional content more quickly or thoroughly. The learners appreciated the additional information that the podcasts provided. The correlation between the four IMMS factors is statistically significant at the 0.01 level, with the strongest relationship being between learner attention and the relevance of the materials and the least strong relationship between the confidence and satisfaction responses. The researchers comment that the positive qualitative results may arise from the fact that podcasts were a novel experience. The 'newness' influence, perhaps also related to the Hawthorne effect (Landsberger, 1958), may produce an increased attentiveness. The question of preferred learning styles (perception modalities) is raised in the discussion.

The lowest scoring area in learner responses is the important aspect of satisfaction. The qualitative responses suggest that file length may be a factor. Learners did not appreciate podcasts lasting for an hour, and the download overheads may have been a distraction. One potentially positive point is that the teachers should refer to the podcasts in the lecture sessions. This would highlight the relevance of the podcasts, raise their status as an integrated resource of the programme and indicate that they are not an optional extra.

What degree of interest (attention) do the learners express?

How pertinent to their situation (relevance) do learners feel?

How much self-assurance (confidence) is expressed by the learners?

What degree of contentment (satisfaction) is expressed by the learners?

What do users like about the technology?

What suggestions for improvement do users have?

Are there differences in response based on: age, gender, social class, cultural background and prior experience?

Source: Based on Bolliger *et al*. (2010: 3)

Figure 2.5 Questioning learners regarding the technology

In this research (Bolliger *et al*., 2010) the podcast is used as an example of a technology supporting learning; the research shows how empirical evidence and rigorous study enhance our understanding of the values of the technology. But the technology must not be the focus. It contains no psychology; it contains no inherent learning. The focus must be on the affordances of that technology and what it can do to enhance learning and to enable learning. As John Potter says in his podcast

> I would encourage them [teachers] to think about subjects and not technology. I would encourage them to think about learners, children and media and not technology. So, not to think about using a short video

clip as an issue of technology but what is in the clip that is going to enhance the literacy learning in the classroom that day, or their knowledge of a different culture ... But the technology doesn't drive it – the desire to make [the learning] be more about popular culture and media now is what drives and enhances that literacy lesson experience for the children. (Potter, 2010)

E-safety in e-learning: safe-working in the virtual world

Technology-enabled learning is not a singular act between a learner and a computer. There are many forms of learning through a computer and the powerful aspect of some of the approaches is the social communication and social constructivism that is enabled. With the ever-growing capacity of computers to connect people there is an increasing capacity for e-safety issues to arise. In Chapter 5 there is a description of e-safety training in action and a commentary on the issues of the ways in which the health and well-being of learners can be protected but, first, what does research tell us about the issues? Some educationalists express the fear that children can both harm others through their use of the computer (Oswell, 1998) and that they can be psychologically harmed (Freeman-Iongo, 2000) by unsupervised access to adult-oriented materials. There are those who would use restrictions of access to reduce risk (discussed by Livingstone and Bober, 2005) and those that promote learners' resilience (Byron, 2008) to meet such challenges. Also, there is disagreement regarding the degree of inappropriate pupil behaviour taking place when they are online. Consequently, the level and the nature of risk that young people are exposed to are not determined.

In the following analysis of research, three areas are considered:

1 What do teachers in training perceive to be the issues?
2 What do the authorities believe is the solution?
3 What do the children say?

The first research to be considered investigates trainee teachers' knowledge and attitudes towards the issues of e-safety. The conclusions are based upon research across four UK higher education institutions and the full study includes: the expert evaluation of a number of e-safety resources; development of an online evaluation form; presenting e-safety sessions to 400 trainee teachers; presenting further resources online and capturing over

73,000 words of comments. The results show that some trainee teachers demonstrate degrees of naivety with regard to e-safety; both positive and negative comments are made and a range of trainee attitudes are expressed. The conclusions drawn from the work inform the way in which we should address issues of e-safety. The elements selected below relate to the psychology aspects of the situation, those pertaining to motivation, under-standing, reflection, morals and ethics (Woollard *et al.*, 2009).

Whilst not all respondents are as passionate, some do make some sensible suggestions including: it is 'the responsibility of ICT technicians to block sites on the internet, Child Protection Officers supporting staff and of course many cite parents and carers for the part that they should play' (Woollard *et al.*, 2007a: 18). They show an understanding of the need to protect pupils' emotional well-being and ability to reflect upon the topic constructively. The trainees make links between their subject specialism and e-safety in creative and thoughtful ways. When asked who they felt should be responsible for dealing with e-safety issues, a majority of the trainees answered in a variety of ways but with one voice, 'everyone' (Woollard *et al.*, 2007a: 17).

The report concludes that there is a need for e-safety training to ensure that teachers in training are adequately prepared to safeguard the pupils for whom they are responsible. The DVD *Jenny's Story* (Childnet, 2005) proved to be a most stimulating resource to focus attention on the issues of e-safety. The evaluation of the impact of *Jenny's Story* as a stimulus to promote discussion and raise awareness, was very compelling, with 84 per cent of the trainees judging themselves to be wiser after the session. As one trainee put it, 'I think this was an excellent video to be shown. The only improvement is to ensure it is shown in as many schools as possible' (Woollard *et al.*, 2007b: 2). Implementing online portals to present advice for tutors, activities for trainees, some classroom resources and information for further study is seen to be an effective way forward.

The second area of research associated with e-safety is the Byron Review. In traditional research terminology, this is considered to be 'critique of the published' evidence. The work is of particular value because of the institutional standing of the author and process and the subsequent widespread dissemination of the findings. The impact of this research report is immense because it was requested by and presented to influential political leaders; the report is widely distributed to and widely respected by the UK education community and the presentation is accessible. In addition, Tanya Byron commissioned three literature reviews on:

1   the effects of video games and the internet on children;
2   children's brain development; and
3   child development (Goswami, 2008).

These reviews informed the report and give the report a strong psychological and evidence-based tone. The psychology of the situation touches
upon behaviour, ethical expectations and morals of the learners. The three
important areas of the psychological dimension (Chapter 1, Figure 1.5) are:
changing attitudes; development and maturity; and satisfaction and motivation. If learners are to be successful in the online environment they must be
prepared and able to handle the technologies, be given the cognitive skills
to assimilate information in the new forms and be resilient to the more
vicarious aspects of the online world.

Changing attitudes

As Tanya Byron reports, research is beginning to reveal that

> people act differently on the internet and can alter their moral code, in
> part because of the lack of gate-keepers and the absence in some cases of
> the visual cues from others that we all use to moderate our interactions
> with each other. This is potentially more complex for children and
> young people who are still trying to establish the social rules of the
> offline world and lack the critical evaluation skills to either be able to
> interpret incoming information or make appropriate judgements about
> how to behave online. (Byron, 2008: 5)

It is important for adults to learn from children and young people themselves, responding to their needs and 'empowering them to take responsibility for their own online behaviours' (Byron, 2008: 109). An important
aspect of changing attitudes is the need for clear ethical instruction and clear
moral guidance. For example, the sexualisation of young people is a
growing concern. 'Sexting' is the activity of sending sexually explicit texts
and/or images by mobile telephone. Often, it is used as confirmation of
relationships but can be employed as acts of victimisation, cyber-bullying
or simply for sexual gratification. This activity is leading to an increased
sexualisation (Zurbriggen *et al.*, 2007) and increased opportunity for
grooming and paedophilia (Powell, 2007).

The learners' responses to exposure to inappropriate material and the impact upon their moral behaviour must have a bearing upon the pedagogic response.

> There is a good chance that young people will access unsuitable materials. They have, of course always been able to find print material which others might deem unsuitable. The difference with the web and email is that some of the material may come looking for them. They may be exposed to material, situations or communications that are undesirable or make them feel uncomfortable. E-safety is everyone's responsibility. (North and McKeown, 2005: 100)

An important element of that inappropriate material is the contact made by cyber-bullies.

Developmental aspects

Tanya Byron reports on the evidence from the child-development and brain-development literature indicating that

> age-related factors and understanding the ways in which children learn can provide a very useful guide to identifying and managing potential risks to children when using the internet or playing video games. (Byron, 2008: 4)

She highlights the importance of the development of the frontal cortex, which mediates their experience and behaviour throughout childhood.

Computer-based game playing is colloquially said to be addictive. It is noted that young people spend more time socialising through the internet using internet messaging and social networking sites. This has lead to concerns about

> excessive use of these technologies by children at the expense of other activities and family interaction. As we increasingly keep our children at home because of fears for their safety outside – in what some see as a 'risk-averse culture' – they will play out their developmental drives to socialize. (Byron, 2008: 3)

Consequently, they may take risks in the digital world where there is little control over the 24-7 access to materials that might negatively effect the younger, developing mind.

Satisfaction/motivation

The developing technology presents users with increasingly immersive experiences, increased vividness and more sophisticated interactions between online players. 'Playing' online games can have a positive cognitive influence (Young *et al.*, 2006) and a positive influence on social development (Yee, 2006). Players can collaborate and form constructive and long-lasting relationships, even to the extent of developing 'second lives' (discussed more fully in Chapter 3, in the section on ID, Id, avatar and persona). Marc Prensky gives an insight into why aspects of games playing are satisfying or motivating (Prensky, 2001c), including the motivational aspects of fun, play, rules (providing structure and security), goals, outcomes and feedback, winning (ego gratification) and more. These are explored Chapter 3 on Theory. Tanya Byron observes that young users' self-developed characters and personalities 'result in new issues related to potentially harmful or inappropriate experiences for children. A recent survey suggested that 25% of players of the massively multiplayer online role-playing games (MMORPGs) are under the age of 18' (Byron, 2008: 156).

Tanya Byron acknowledges that debates and research in this area can be highly polarised. This is particularly evident in areas such as the impact of, say, violent imagery on the behaviour of young people. Research is a continuing theme through the report, with commentary on the evidence but acknowledgement that there is insufficient research in this area. However, researching the effects of inappropriate material on children can be particularly problematic ethically. Research and teachers' actions in this area can develop our understanding.

> To help us measure and manage those risks [harm from video games and use of the internet] we need to focus on what the child brings to the technology and use our understanding of children's development to inform an approach that is based on the 'probability of risk' in different circumstances. (Byron, 2009: 3)

The mixed research evidence on the activities does not mean that the risks do not exist but it is likely that the context of the activity and the individual child's characteristics will have a greater influence on the effects of the activity than the activity itself. For example, children from more deprived backgrounds may be more at risk online because of a lack of confidence with new technology or because their parents are less likely to be engaged with their children's use of the internet. These are important issues of social justice. Further information about the digital divide and the impact of social background, gender and age on computer usage and online behaviour can be found at http://www.ukonlinecentres.com.

The final area of research associated with e-safety focuses on the attitudes towards and perceptions of risk in online activities by primary school-aged children. The study by Sue Cranmer, Neil Selwyn and John Potter gathers empirical data from over 600 children attending five different primary schools and creates a picture of the perceived issues of ICT. The researchers identify four research questions:

1 'How do pupils understand and talk about issues of safety and risk with regard to ICTs?
2 How do these understandings differ by gender, age and school attended?
3 How do concerns with safety and risk influence pupils' engagement with ICTs?
4 What implications does this have for the ongoing "e-safety" agenda in schools and home?' (Cranmer et al., 2009: 130).

There are four very important aspects of this research that should be acknowledged:

1 The focus of attention is on young children, aged 7 to 11, whereas previous attention in the area of e-safety has been on the behaviours and attitudes of older pupils and adolescents.
2 The research endeavours to hear the 'pupil voice'.
3 The research methodological approach uses a constant comparative (grounded theory) technique to analyse the qualitative data gained through questionnaire and focus group discussions.
4 The research method employed trained children to act as the researcher in focussing the discussion groups.

Their research leads them to conclude that teachers need to refocus the way in which e-safety is taught and they suggest

the introduction of media literacy programmes which embed safety guidance within a wider reflection on technology use. It is conceivable that current 'bolt-on' or stand-alone e-safety initiatives are seen by children as a 'dampener' on their enthusiasms for digital technologies. By embedding these messages within more positive approaches which seek to develop children's skills, knowledge and confidence with ICTs more generally, a more equitable balance of positive and negative is achieved. (Cranmer *et al.*, 2009: 140)

They also identify the fact that the pupils are affected by exaggerated fears (Selwyn *et al.*, 2009). Perhaps the tone of the professional dialogue around e-safety should be considered.

Summary

The range and diversity of research relating to technology-enabled teaching, independent online learning and the technology itself is great. The resulting descriptions of practice and their efficacy are therefore often difficult to compare. Through the large-scale meta-analysis processes we begin to see the 'big picture', the trends and the patterns. There is strong evidence that technology is having an impact upon how well we teach, both in terms of efficacy and in terms of entitlement and opportunity for all. There is growing evidence of the change in learning patterns and how learners learn. This chapter has introduced the key elements of research in the field of technology-enabled teaching: meta-analysis and critique and the key areas for investigation, the ways of learning, the context for learning and the technology of teaching.

Activities

- Consider, in the light of the content of the chapter, the different areas of your own practice where e-learning has the greatest impact upon the nature and efficacy of your teaching. What is the nature of that impact? Is it social, curriculum or technology based?
- Consider the different approaches to research and which are more influential on your beliefs about the values of technology in teaching and learning.
- Identify the values of meta-analysis and critique and how the conclusions of individual research projects might be better judged.
- Identify the key issues of e-safety that relate to the learners for whom you are responsible.

3 Theory

By the end of this chapter you will be:

- able to identify the important theoretical areas related to technology-enabled teaching;
- aware of the diversity of theoretical constructs that underpin the use of technology in education;
- able to relate developmental theory of cognition to the appropriate use of technology; and
- able to identify the importance of personality theory in understanding activities of avatars in virtual worlds.

Technology-enabled teaching and learning are associated with a diverse range of underpinning theoretical viewpoints including: learning, personality, motivation or developmental theories focussing on the learner. Theoretical constructs relating to the teacher and teaching include the behaviourist design of software, stages of online interactivity of tutors and levels of teacher engagement in virtual worlds. This chapter begins by considering the developmental theories.

Stages of cognitive development

Jean Piaget (1896–1980) has been influential in establishing hierarchies of development guiding classroom design, curriculum content, teaching methods and the understanding of changes as children grow towards adolescence. His work focuses on brain development in childhood and how a child's thinking changes with maturation. His theory of cognitive development brings understanding of constructivist learning. It can be applied to the field of e-learning and perhaps bring a better understanding of what e-learning is all about.

Piaget proposed stages of cognitive development; these can be interpreted in terms of computer-based activities and exemplified by common classroom practice. In Table 3.1 the stages (age ranges) have been selected to best reflect the changes in the potential of the child to participate in activities of computer-based learning and parallel Piaget's model of the developing brain and ways of thinking.

Table 3.1 Stages of cognitive development

Piaget stages	Age	Piaget's concepts	Computer-based activities	Examples discussed
Sensori-motor	up to 2 years	reflex activity, repetition, egocentrism, object permanence	key, button and switch tapping; responding to images, light, colour and sound	Voice and sound boxes used by those with special educational needs – an older child operating as a two-year-old
Pre-operational (symbolic function)	2 to 4 years	representation (of objects/actions by language and image), animism	key press associated with activity	MULCH, Beebot
Pre-operational (intuitive)	4 to 7 years	social speech, focus (centration), judgement, basic rules	sorting, binary tree, searching, rote learning	switch friendly games, Roamer, interactive whiteboard, ReTreeval
Concrete operations	7 to 11 years	conservation, seriation (ordering), classification, logic, reversibility, number, space, time and speed	presentations, sequencing, complex search criteria, Boolean operators	Roamer, LOGO, DataSweet, searching on the internet
Formal operations	11 to 15 years	proportion, proposition (hypothetical), double systems, equilibrium, probability, elasticity and regulation	modelling, programming, algorithm, representations	Scratch, spreadsheets, simulations, expert systems

Source: Based on Piaget (1929/1964).

The computer-enhanced learning by infants up to the age of two is very much based on electronic toys of the 'touch and respond' type. Some devices respond to sound – clap and they play. For example, Leapfrog My Pal Scout toddler toy,

> is an interactive companion that helps children (toddlers) to learn with an entertaining twist ... is an electronic learning toy ... between the ages of six months to three years ... music, lights, and singsong voice ... can be personalized to your child ... connect to the online ... [includes] three 'AAA' batteries, one USB cable. (Baby Toys, 2010)

These learning activites could be interpreted as purely behaviourist in nature. The infant makes a gesture and is rewarded; like the pigeons in many of Skinner's experiments, the infant is being subjected to operant conditioning. The infant's actions are reinforced and they occur more frequently until saturation occurs. The infant is acting at the sensori-motor stage.

As the infant develops into the pre-operational (symbolic) stage, there is more precision and an association between different responses and the reactions they cause. The basic programmable toys have a one-to-one relationship between the buttons and their actions. For example, a favourite toy of my children in the 1980s was MULCH, a robot gardener. It has nine buttons, one for each action: lights flash, turn in a circle, dance (turning left and right in rapid succession), forward, backward, sing (a simple monochromatic tune) and go. At three years of age, the learning activity was press and see the response; from four years old, it was putting the actions together in a sequence.

From four years old to seven years old children are in the pre-operational (intuitive) stage and are able to put together sequences of events. It is common practice in early years and infants classes to use devices like the Valient Roamer (Piper, 2000; Valient, 2010). To make the Roamer move, the child enters a sequence of instructions. The three key presses [^] [5] [GO] makes the Roamer go forward five paces (five Roamer lengths). It would be expected that seven-year-olds would be able to construct sequences of instructions with iteration and calls to procedures that they had previously made.

> The evidence would certainly indicate that it is an excellent tool for use within the classroom. The children enjoy lessons using Roamer (as based on my own observations) and, used imaginatively, Roamer can assist in the teaching and learning of many mathematical concepts. Introducing

Roamer into mathematics lessons can provide opportunities for investigation, encourage mathematical discussion and generally make mathematics more practical and enjoyable. (Piper, 2000)

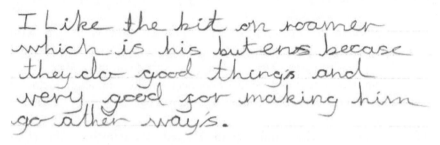

I Like the bit on roamer which is his butens becase they do good things and very good for making him go other ways.

Figure 3.1 Reflections of a six-year-old on using a Roamer

From the motivational and emotional perspective of learning, at this stage children have more difficulty separating pretence from reality, especially scary pretence (Harris *et al.*, 1991). Content is potentially more frightening for younger children as it is likely to have a more significant impact on their ability to process it without distress. 'Just as with other kinds of media content, we need an age-related approach when thinking about appropriateness of content within video games for children, with younger children protected from extreme content that may cause them harm' (Byron, 2008: 151). Even innocent games, such as *Granny's Garden*, can have an effect upon children. (See the 'emotional engagement' section of Chapter 4 on Pedagogy.)

The pre-operational intuitive stage accommodates the organisation of objects into sets following basic rules. The learners can explore structures, but for them to independently classify objects and create sequences based on the individual object's properties they must have moved on to the concrete operations stage. The cognition behind the physical activities of classifying, sorting and sequencing are supported by computer software. For example, ReTreeval (Kudlian, 2008) is designed to make the connection between prose questions such as 'Is it blue?' 'What shape is it?' and the methodical organisation of the data, based on a tree structure, in a database management system.

The other aspects of the concrete stage are seriation (ordering), classification and logic. These are also supported by data-handling software. Charting programs enable children to enter data and immediately see the graph, in the form of bar charts, pie charts, line graphs, histograms or scattergrams. Flat file databases give learners the opportunity to associate several

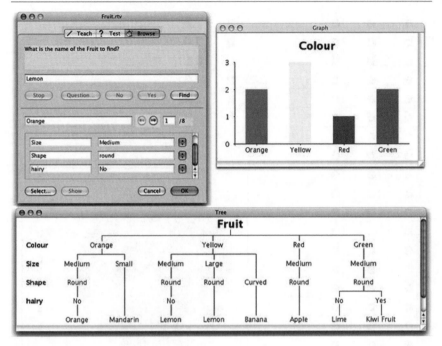

Source: From http://www.kudlian.net.

Figure 3.2 ReTreeval software for creating tree data structures

characteristics (fields) with each object (record). Then, by sorting and searching, they can discover patterns.

The highest stage of Piaget's cognitive development – formal operations – is reflected in the use of basic office-type software but in increasingly sophisticated ways. The most flexible application is the spreadsheet.

Proportion – using a spreadsheet 'count if' function on an area of values/ qualities and then charting the totals for each value/quality gives a visual and interactive display of proportionality. Knowledge, represented as an array of facts, is converted to visual imagery, represented by a pie chart.

Double systems – the 'classification of elements in a double entry table' (Inhelder and Piaget, 1958: 312). The simplest forms are scattergram, Carroll diagram, logic table and Venn diagram. The scattergram has a variable measure for each axis and the entry is a star. The pattern formed by those stars indicates the relation (correlation) between the variables on the axes. The Carroll diagram has states and not-state on the axes and the entries in the table are items corresponding to that state. The logic table has true or false (logic) or a statement of the inter-connection. The Venn diagram has overlapping circles (sets) with items falling into the overlap if

a	a	e		a	3		
b	c	e		b	14		
c	b	d		c	11		
e	e	c		d	4		
e	e	b		e	22		
d	d	c		f	0		
c	c	b					
b	b	e					
e	e	e					
a	c	b					
c	b	e					
b	e	e					
e	c	b					
e	b	e					
d	e	e					
c	c	b					
b	b	e					
e	e	e					

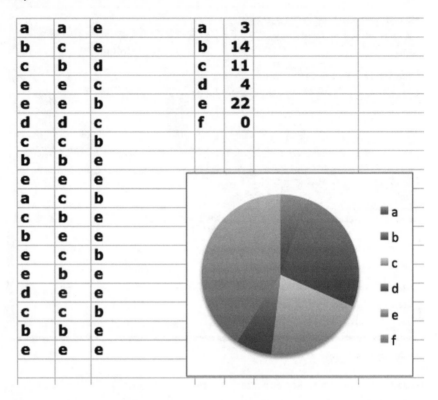

Figure 3.3 Using technology to explore proportion more thoroughly

they are members of both sets. These different forms of pictorial graphics are needed to represent the different way in which information can be visualised mentally. Some of these technology-enabled devices can aid the gestalt (Ellis, 1938) mental visualisation process.

Equilibrium – one aspect of equilibrium is the intersection between two formulae; for example, the formula for the income from sales of one to many items and the formula for the costs of manufacture of one to many items. When these are plotted together on a chart they show the breakeven point. Another graphical representation easily achieved using technology is plotting the cooling curves of hot substances in a cooler environment, such as 'in a science experiment, the temperature of a cup of coffee is measured over half an hour' (DfES, 2004c: 15). These two examples barely scratch the surface of the equilibrium construct (Inhelder and Piaget, 1958) which includes: equality (140); representation (187); stability (258); physical (319); psychological (258). However, there are clear examples of areas where technology-enhanced teaching is more effective in portraying the concepts of, in these cases, commerce and physical sciences. The computer imagery

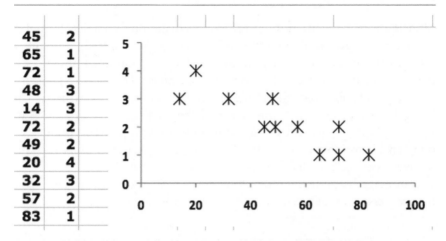

45	2
65	1
72	1
48	3
14	3
72	2
49	2
20	4
32	3
57	2
83	1

Figure 3.4 Scattergram showing the relationship between two values from each member of a set

acts as a metaphor for the concept. The intersection of two lines at a precise point on the screen is a visual metaphor representing the breakeven point on a profit/loss chart, which is a theoretical construct.

Proposition (hypothetical) – asking the 'what if' question when exploring a model. The cognitively most sophisticated and engaging activity with a computer can be considered to be modelling. From *Learning and Teaching Using ICT*:

> Modelling is an important aspect of the ICT curriculum and it provides important strategies for helping students understand scientific concepts and relationships. Students can use ICT to create models and explore understanding by asking 'what if' questions. They can modify rules and variables to explore the relationships within the model, predict outcomes and test hypotheses. The models can be presented as spreadsheets of data. Alternatively, the numbers can be embedded into multimedia presentations and interactive applications; for example, wave simulation programs that allow the students to explore amplitude, frequency and direction when combining, passing through a refraction grating or being reflected off a solid surface. (Woollard, 2007a: 172)

Modelling has two aspects:

1 modelling is the use of models – exploration and investigation of simulations, spreadsheets, expert systems and charting programs; and
2 modelling is the creation of models through designing spreadsheets, writing computer programs or authoring in a computer environment.

Models are representations of a real world situation by variables, formulae and relationships, usually in a spreadsheet or, more graphically, through a microworld or simulation. The learner is able to set up situations and see the consequences of their decisions. For example, *The Model Shop* from Sherston Software poses the challenge 'Simulation Street is in danger of being destroyed, and only computer modelling skills can save the day! Can your pupils help Josie, armed only with her trusty laptop, to sort out everyone's problems?' (Sherston, 2010). Learners use higher level thinking skills to investigate and then hypothesise.

Jean Piaget's construct of developmental stages has a clear parallel with the progression in the use of computer-based teaching devices.

An educational software paradigm

Behaviourism is a philosophy, theory and pedagogy supported by empirical data obtained through careful and controlled scrutiny and measurement of observable behaviour under laboratory conditions or within well-defined social environments, such as the classroom, work place, community and home.

A formal description of behaviourism

Behaviourism asserts that there are *direct parallels between animals and humans* in the way in which learning appears to occur and that valuable research can be carried out on animals as well as humans.

Behaviourism asserts that *from conception* the mind is influenced by the environment and experiences and that the environment, experiences and the actions of other people influence a person's *motivation* and *behaviour*.

Behaviourism asserts that all behaviour, no matter how complex, can be reduced to a simple *stimulus–response* association and new behaviour occurs through: *classical or operant conditioning*; or the *modification* of old behaviour through *rewards* and punishments; or imitation of observed behaviour called *modelling*. Rewards are more effective than punishments.

Behaviourism accepts that some rewards are *intrinsic* and associated with internal senses of gratification (pleasure), well-being (absence of need) or moral correctness (righteousness) and that the outcomes of some internal processes (such as learning) evoke those rewards.

> Behaviourism encompasses aspects of *affective domain* that are reflected in the physical domain (interest, curiosity, motivation, cooperation, attitude, belief) and that these behaviours are influenced by reward and punishment. (Woollard, 2010: 21–22)

Many approaches to computer-based teaching and training are founded on this philosophy. There is a rich and valued history of effective teaching with computers underpinned by the behaviourist approach.

B.S. Skinner's programmed learning theory (Skinner, 1954) led to the development of the teaching machine based on the strategies of task analysis, the sequencing of learning and the presentation of the concepts through small steps with positive reinforcement as each step is successfully negotiated. The following description is taken from *Walden Two*.

> In this device, [teaching machine] a human learner is given a logically connected series of questions or problems, to each of which there is one correct answer from among the alternative answers offered by the machine. If the learner selects a wrong answer, the machine provides an explanation of the error and directs the student back to a clarifying point in the sequence. If the learner selects the right answer, the machine tells him that he is right and sends him on to the next question. (Skinner, 1948: 6–7)

This approach remains both efficient in presenting teaching materials and effective through motivating and enabling the learners. It is particularly applicable where the computer-enabled learning is undertaken by a single learner working without the direct (synchronous) support of a tutor or the social support of fellow learners.

During the 1980s, the media-enhanced applications of HyperCard and presentation software enabled content designers to enrich the learning experience. Real places and events could be represented on screen by low-fidelity video imagery of the real or simulated graphics to represent the real. This enabled the learner to be more engaged in the process and made the rewards more motivating. At the highest level of sophistication of computer-based modelling are flight-training simulators, where the fidelity approaches 100 per cent. From a technical viewpoint, the capsule that contains the flight deck simulator, the screens that show the images and the location of the apparatus are far from being a real aeroplane. However, the immersive effects of the indicative visual imagery, the reinforcement of the kinaesthetic through switches and the physical orientation/sensation, the narrative of the experience and the emotional engagement in the process mean that trainee pilots experience a near 100 per cent fidelity. The psychological involvement is so great that both trainee and experienced pilots need to be debriefed and pastorally supported after making a mistake whilst 'flying the aircraft'. In the classroom, the fidelity is far lower but can still achieve immersion. (See the 'emotional engagement' section of Chapter 4 on Pedagogy.)

The look-and-say phonics approaches, the chanting of times tables and the rote learning of facts and figures up until the 1970s had a significant influence on the design of computer software for the early classroom-based computers. Then, technology-enabled learning focussed on spelling, numeracy and facts and figures. There were right and wrong answers. Buzzes, bells and simple graphics rewarded the right answers. Wrong responses were greeted with a repeated question. Scoring and league tables were features of the positive feedback and encouragement built into the programs.

Although programmed learning machines are no longer used, they are emulated in the structures of some computer-based applications, such as the integrated learning systems (ILS). In the 1980s, they were developed to provide individualised, measured and controlled teaching experiences in the basic skills of numeracy and literacy. They remain an effective approach to this day, being based on networked computers providing instructional content as well as assessment and learning management tools. Instruction is organised around specific objectives and the software is based on a mastery learning approach to instruction, whereby learners do not advance to the next learning objective until they achieve proficiency in the current one. The principles are founded on the implications of reinforcement theory (Markle, 1969; Skinner, 1968) and require the curriculum to be presented as a series of frames. A current example is SuccessMaker® (Pearson, 2009).

Stages of online interactivity

Understanding the value of computers in teaching and learning and the widespread access to internet-connected computers came together in the late 1990s. Models of working were being established and computer-mediated activities in education started to become collaborative, interactive, focussed and analysed. Research by Gráinne Conole (Conole, 2007; Conole and Oliver, 2007), Diana Laurillard (Laurillard, 2002), Bridget Somekh (Somekh, 2007), Etienne Wenger (Wenger et al., 2002; 2009) and Gilly Salmon (Salmon, 2000) moved the agenda of online learning into the social dimension. The term 'communities of practice' (CoP) has been established to describe the interaction between people who have a common goal in learning, either formal or informal. Etienne Wenger describes communities of practice as 'groups of people who share a concern or a passion for something they do and learn how to do it better as they interact regularly' (Wenger, 2006). He describes the construct of community of practice as requiring three elements: domain, community and practice. The domain is the focus, the community is the group of identified people participating and the practice is the engagement activities of those people. 'They develop a shared repertoire of resources: experiences, stories, tools, ways of addressing recurring problems – in short a shared practice' (Wenger, 2006).

One theoretical model that emerged brought understanding to the process of individuals' maturity in the process of using computers in learning. Gilly Salmon created a model through detailed analysis of participants' online conversations. 'This analysis [coding the statements of participants] led me to revise the categorizations of some messages, and to a greater sense of the sequence of activities pursued by the online participants' (Salmon, 2000: 25). The resulting five-step model is a useful way of analysing and describing an e-learner's maturation in a number of learning situations. It describes the increasing level of interactivity through the stages of:

■ access and motivation;
■ online socialisation;
■ information exchange;
■ knowledge construction;
■ [learner] development.

The model also shows the balance between the activity of what Gilly Salmon termed, the 'e-moderator' and the activities of technical support (Salmon, 2000: 26). The table below applies the Salmon model to the stages through which learning avatars develop in an immersive virtual world. There are direct parallels with the 'social domain of the blended taxonomy' (Scopes, 2009), which includes personalising, contextualising, communicating, affiliating, networking and channelling and is described later in this chapter.

In the final stage, 'participants become responsible for their own learning through computer-mediated opportunities and need little support beyond that already available' (Salmon, 2000: 35). Independent learning and a sense of value and self-control liberates many and secures their life-long learning through the media of computers. In the more detailed account of the

Table 3.2 Five-stage model of learning and socialisation in a virtual world

Access and motivation	Online socialisation	Information exchange	Knowledge construction	Learner development
by:	by:	by:	by:	by:
building a platform associated with an island and adding the facilities of: SLurls; notice cards; Welcome Points; dexterity training	ensuring identities are known; using IM and local chat; creating groups; creating mail lists;	creating notice boards; easels; presentations and setting targets including peregrination, treasure hunts and guided tours	developing conferencing facilities/skills; scheduling events and meetings; creating interactive learning resources including out-of-world blogs, wikis and forum	building networks; promoting friendships outside the group; supporting exploration; celebrating achievements ...
and so:	and so:	and so:	and so:	and so:
enabling access and stimulating motivation through successful navigation and providing a sense of safety (home).	promoting online socialisation; creating the foundations for collaboration and cooperation; and developing socialisation skills.	enabling learners to gather information; report their findings and be aware of others' work.	enabling shared and agreed constructs of learning.	establishing full immersion in the virtual world, confidence in exploration and competence to assimilate and communicate information.

Source: Based on Salmon (2000) and Scopes (2009).

five-stage model, three separate activities of 'advice on technical support ... helping participant to learn [motivating] and ... e-moderating' are detailed (Salmon, 2000: 115–119).

Learning in cyberspace

The final theoretical consideration is the concept of cybergogy. As discussed in the section 'Towards a definition of e-learning', there is a very general use of the word 'cybergogy' which encompasses all forms of peda-gogy that are technology-enabled. However, there are advocates of the idea that cybergogy only applies to teaching and learning within a virtual world. Virtual worlds, as an emerging platform for teaching and learning, require a more specialised instructional design approach if they are to demonstrate their potential to move e-teaching away from classical methods of online delivery of education and training. It is this aspect of pedagogy that is now described. Table 3.3 identifies the terminology and indicates where some words are used synonymously and where there are nuances of difference in meaning.

Table 3.3 Terminology of cybergogy

Cybergogy	The pedagogy of the virtual world
Avatar	A digital representation of himself, herself or other self in the form of a three-dimensional animated agent whose actions, interactions and decisions are under the control of the learner.
Virtual world	A visual and audio representation of a computer-generated persistent location wherein avatars can interact with the environment and with other learners' avatars.
3Di	Three-dimensional immersive application that affects human senses via visual and auditory means to create an ambience.
Microworld	First coined in the 1970s, a virtual world that can be explored with activities like *Granny's Garden* and LOGO programming but without the user avatar.
Metaverse	The network of 3D virtual worlds that is expanded when new 3D worlds are added. Term coined in *Snow Crash* by Neil Stephenson (1992).
Flatland	A pejorative term for the 2D presentation of learning materials such as conventional learning platforms, the 2D web and VLEs.
3DLE	A virtual world designed specifically with the goal of learning.
Second Life®	A social-centric virtual world supporting leisure, business and educational activity. Not necessarily designed for learning, some users are actively customising parts as a learning platform.
Learning archetype	Pedagogic metaphors and fundamental tools of cybergogy; these are classifications of activities that maximise the essence of a virtual world, in as much as its ability to facilitate learning experiences is delimited by physical world constraints.
Learning domains	Aspects of sentience which can be addressed in combinations to provide learning experiences.

Current academic research in the area of virtual worlds focuses upon the impact of the immersive nature of virtual world experience (Book, 2006; De Lucia *et al.*, 2008; Doyle, 2010; Malaby, 2007), the developing curriculum application (Mallan *et al.*, 2010) and the implications for global access (Hunsinger and Krotoski, 2010). This section describes a pedagogy, called cybergogy, that is specifically designed for the virtual world, based on the work of Lesley Scopes (Scopes, 2009) that was acknowledged as a detailed approach by Karl Kapp and Tony O'Driscoll in their book *Learning in 3D* (Kapp and O'Driscoll, 2010). It is structured on the premise of the social constructivist view of learning, where knowledge is constructed and internalised by the learner and is sustained by social processes. The model of cybergogy that follows is based on the development of these ideas.

ID, Id, avatar and persona: the changing face of self

An avatar is a person's representation of himself or herself within a computer system. The definition of avatar begins by stating what it is not – it is not a real person. Jeremy Bailenson and Kathryn Segovia use the term 'doppelganger' (Bailenson and Segovia, 2010: 175) to indicate both the connection but also the separation of self from the avatar. The rules, principles and theories of human psychology do not automatically apply to the behaviours of the avatar but, with an ever-increasing fidelity of representation and with an ever-increasing immersive nature of the virtual environment, we are witnessing characteristics of behaviour of avatars that have striking parallels with the behaviours of humans in real-world situations and, importantly, the behaviours and characteristics of the avatars are not the same as the person driving the avatar. This section explores a major theory of personality and then considers other views in relation to the appearance, behaviour and apparent motivations of avatars in the immersive 3D environment.

The human body carries out three functions in the social world – communication, representation and peregrination. It is through our bodies that we communicate with others by gesture, action and word. It is through our bodies and the way in which we dress and adorn our bodies that we represent ourselves and our status within the society in which we live. And, by means of our bodies we move about our environment, going to places and meeting people. Avatars in learning environments have three parallel functions of supporting communication, representation and peregrination. The first characteristic of the avatar to be determined is their ID or identification. In the popular virtual world Second Life® (Linden Lab, 2010), the second name has to be chosen from a relatively narrow set of names on offer at the time of 'birth' (registration). An avatar's age is given in years and months from the moment of becoming a resident. The owner then gives a first name of their choice. The only identity connection between the real person and the avatar is the email address required by Linden Labs as some form of authentication. For most users there is a feeling of connection between themselves and their avatar and it will be a representation of themselves and their id. The next stage is usually to modify the appearance of the avatar and, since this is under the control of the learner, the process of personalisation and moving the ID of the avatar closer to the Id the learner wishes to present (or subconsciously presents) can begin.

Communication

The avatar is the focus of all communication. People can only 'hear' the avatar if they are physically close, the volume decreases as they walk away; others can only see the local chat if they are in the same environment, and IM at a distance is identified by the name of the avatar, not the person.

Communication is also in the form of gestures such as whistle, clap, nod and shake.

Representation

The avatar represents the person without there being direct communication. It is what they look like in profiles and when present in the learning environment.

The psychology associated with 'judging on appearance' comes into play.

Peregrination

The avatar is the location. All views the learner has of the world occur in relation to the avatar. The learner cannot be in one place and see what is happening in another.

Peregrination, the ability to move quickly and efficiently from one place to another is an essential aspect of the learning experience.

Figure 3.5 The three functions of avatars

Sigmund Freud proposed a number of life instincts that determine the behaviour of a person and that these are reflected as the persona. These theoretical constructs included the libido, related to the sexual instinct required for the reproduction and, therefore, future success of the species. Some relate to the survival of the individual and are connected to the lower order Maslow 'needs' and instincts. Others include the basic drives (or primary processes) such as pleasure and passion. These are collectively called the 'Id'. The 'Ego' is the more pragmatic aspect of the subconscious, motivated by operating in relation to the outside world through the 'akust' (cap of hearing). The drives of the Id are modified by the impact of the external world through the perceptual consciousness and cap of hearing. They are also reduced by what Freud calls *verdrängte* – repression.

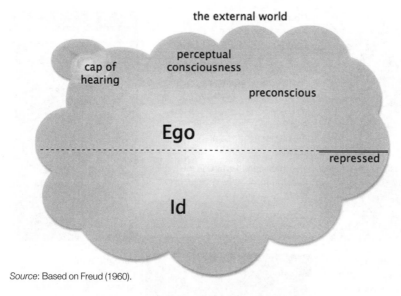

Source: Based on Freud (1960).

Figure 3.6 Classical hierarchical diagram

As people reinvent themselves through their avatar we can suppose that the avatar will be subconsciously affected by the Id through the Ego. That is, the degree to which the individual's desires are impacted upon by social conventions of the virtual world, repression of basic desires and the pragmatism of the Ego to succeed in the long-term. Tansley, in his book *The New Psychology and Its Relation to Life*, calls these the 'herd complex', the 'sex complex' and the 'ego complex'. Tansley makes a clear statement about human desire and the

> importance and universality of the processes by which the mind seeks, more or less successfully, to escape from the discomforting realization of its own weakness and from the conflicts engendered by opposed instincts, as well as from the disharmony of a chaotic world. (Tansley, 1920: 183)

As we see people attracted to the virtual worlds and investing in and developing their avatars, we need to be aware of the conscious and subconscious motivations that result in avatars that sometimes represent the learner accurately, imaginatively, ideally and controversially. Mark Meadows in *I, Avatar* makes the claim that '75 percent of Internet users feel safer speaking their mind when they use an avatar' (Meadows, 2008: 36). Perhaps this is an indication that the Ego is being more strongly driven by the Id when the Ego is working in the less oppressive environment of the virtual world. Current work by Howard Gardner, including the GoodPlay Project, explores the development of ethics by young people and how 'ethical minds' are developed in the new media. He recognises identity, privacy, ownership and authorship, credibility, and participation as key elements of the developing self (Gardner, 2008). Another approach to examining the way in which avatars behave is to consider their moral characteristics identified through their behaviours. Lawrence Kohlberg's stages of moral development, developed over his lifetime, are based on a similar developmental structure to that of Jean Piaget's cognitive stages. The theory postulates six identifiable developmental stages of growth, in which the person is better able to handle moral dilemmas based on the concept of justice and ethics, the further they proceed through the stages.

There are important implications arising from the consideration of Lawrence Kohlberg's stages of moral development (Kohlberg, 1975: 671) with regard to pedagogy and technology-enabled learning. The least mature learners may disclose personal information and put themselves at risk and the learners may do things thinking they are protected by the false identity or avatar. More mature learners may become vulnerable because they take risks or break local rules that do not comply with their morals or the ethical context in which they usually work.

Another way of analysing personality is by considering the outward expressions, assertions and behaviours or avatars. The 'Big Five' is a popular procedure for classifying personality types (John and Srivastava, 1999). It was originally derived in the 1970s by psychologists at the National Institutes of Health and, independently, by Warren Norman and Lewis Goldberg. They established, through a grounded theory approach (building a theory from data and then collecting and re-analysing more data until the theory does not change), that most human personality traits can be boiled down to five broad areas, regardless of language or culture, represented by these constructs:

1   closed-minded – open to new experiences;
2   disorganised – conscientious;
3   introverted – extraverted;
4   disagreeable – agreeable;
5   calm/relaxed – nervous/high-strung.

Table 3.4 Moral development and response to ethics in learning environments

Kohlberg's stages of moral development	Behaviours in the flatlands of social networking, chat room, forum and virtual learning environments	Additional behaviours in the 3D immersive environments	Cautions for the e-tutor, e-trainer and e-teacher
Level 1 (Pre-Conventional) Stage 1 – Obedience and punishment	following instructions exactly, such as 'Zip it, Block it, Flag it'; providing full and correct identity; disclosing personal information on request; reading and being conscious of 'terms and conditions'	making the avatar match themselves; being and doing in the virtual world as they think they are and do in the real world; never breaking the rules	learners may disclose personal information and put themselves at risk
Level 1 (Pre-Conventional) Stage 2 – Self-interest	choosing the option best for them; thinking that breaking some rules may be acceptable; considering using a pseudonym	hiding behind the avatar name	these learners may do things thinking they are protected by the false identity or avatar
Level 2 (Conventional) Stage 3 – Interpersonal accord and conformity	arguing that someone can be good if, when they break rules, they do it for good reasons; disclosing others' and their own misdemeanours because they feel they are right; rationalised and therefore condoning rule-breaking if they feel it fits within the ethical rules (their morals); not fully complying with rules they see as unfair (for example, copying text for their assignments)	making the avatar do things that certain others may feel is wrong; learner may suffer abuse or disapproval from residents if they do not conform (for example, placing themselves physically between two avatars in conversation)	these learners may become vulnerable because they knowingly take risks or because they break local rules that do not comply with their own morals or the ethical context in which they usually work

Level 2 (Conventional) Stage 4 – Maintaining social order	working towards the notion of a good society; supporting procedures put in place to protect ('Zip it, Block it, Flag it' and CEOP Report button)	building rules for their communities; developing a policing strategy	these are competent e-learners; they will be working in safe ways and ensuring that others are safe
	seeing the need to protect individual rights; defending others within online communities;		
	settling disputes through democratic processes; participating in open (chat room) debate about moral dilemmas		
Level 3 (Post-Conventional) Stage 5 – Social contract orientation	challenging the conventions when they feel the conventions are not in the interest of all; protecting the oppressed minority		
Level 3 (Post-Conventional) Stage 6 – Universal ethical principles	expressing a principled conscience in online chats		

Source: Based on Kohlberg (1975).

They are often referred to as the OCEAN model of personality, based on the acronym derived form the names of the five dimensions.

The value of this, or any other personality construct, in helping us understand the behaviours and motivations of avatars in virtual worlds, is expressed by this observation on personnel selection by Lewis Goldberg's writing,

> Back in the days when we had no personalities [personality tests], it made no sense to use personality measures in personnel selection [identifying avatars]. Now that we have regained our personalities, evidence has been accruing about the utility of personality measures as predictors of diverse criteria. Recently ... reviews of the literature have concluded that personality measures, when classified within the Big-Five domains, are systematically related to a variety of criteria of job performance [avatar role]. (Goldberg, 1993: 31)

He goes on to discuss the merits of the 'conscientiousness' trait with regard to job performance. In the field of technology-enabled learning, conscientiousness is likely to be an important trait to identify; however, the values of openness are also important if the avatar is to represent an imaginative,

Table 3.5 Traits of personality of the Big Five taxonomy

O	openness	original, inventive, creative, curious, complex, adventurous, interest in art/aesthetics/emotion	conventional, consistent, down to earth, incurious, narrow interests, uncreative
C	conscientiousness	reliable, well-organized, self-disciplined, careful	disorganized, undependable, negligent
E	extraversion	surgency, seeking stimulation, outgoing, energetic, sociable, friendly, fun-loving, competitive, talkative, proactive, dominating, self-confident, decisive, frank, quick to positive emotions, cheerful, happy	introverted, reserved, inhibited, quiet
A	agreeableness	friendly, compassionate, good-natured, sympathetic, forgiving, courteous, cooperative	competitive, outspoken, critical, suspicious, callous, rude, harsh, antagonistic, irritable
N	neuroticism		feeling of vulnerability, nervous, anxious, high-strung, insecure, worrying, tense, quick to fear, anger and dislike, depressed

creative and lateral thinker. The social element of online learning situations also makes the agreeableness trait an important factor in successful collaborative and cooperative learning.

More recent research in the field of avatar behaviours considers how they 'touch' each other (haptic interaction) in the virtual world. A haptic interface is a force-reflecting device that allows a user to touch, feel, manipulate, create and/or alter simulated 3D objects in a virtual environment. Those objects can be other avatars. Jeremy Bailenson examined the manners in which avatars touch digital representations of other avatars (Baileson and Lee, 2007), comparing it to the manner in which they touch digital representations of objects. He observed that avatars use less force when touching other avatars than objects, and those avatars touched the face with less force than the torso area. He also notes that male digital representations were touched with more force than female representations by avatars of both genders. These haptic studies add one more facet to the world of avatars that needs a deeper theoretical understanding so that the pedagogy is better established. They show that there are correlations between behaviours of avatars and human behaviours. However, we also know that people act differently online than they do in physical settings. They do and say things online that they would not do offline; adults and children, who are already vulnerable in the online environments, put themselves at greater risks. They do not necessarily behave well in deed and word, including in such areas as:

- cyber-flirting (Whitty, 2003);
- risk taking (Byron, 2008: 56);
- meeting offline (Livingstone and Helsper, 2007);
- role/gender experimentation (Richards, 2009);
- virtual physical contact (Bailenson and Yee, 2007);
- false memories in children (Segovia and Bailenson, 2009); and
- truth and lying (Whitty and Joinson, 2008).

Summary

The theoretical basis for supporting the use of technology in education arises from a diverse range of disciplines, including cognitive development psychology, personality theory and motivation theory. The learning theories find their influence in many areas of technology-enabled teaching: behaviourism with feedback, reward and task analysis of the curriculum, constructionism through authoring and programming in computer environments, constructivism through social networking and Web 2.0 applications and cognitivism through mindtools, information processing and problem solving. Other theoretical approaches describe the underpinning ideas of pedagogy, andragogy and cybergogy. This chapter has introduced the key areas of theory in the field of technology-enabled teaching: stages of cognitive development, the design of software, the value of interactivity, engagement and immersion and the role of self in the way in which learners behave online.

Activities

- Consider, in the light of the content of this chapter, the different theoretical viewpoints and which you judge the most influential on your practice: learning, personality, motivation or developmental theories.
- Consider the model of online interactivity (Table 3.2) and determine your personal level of engagement with technology in teaching; if you are working in a virtual world, then consider the degree of that engagement.
- Consider how you represent yourself (or will represent yourself) in a virtual world; what do you feel will be the differences between who you are and the impression that your avatar, its actions and communication will give?

4

Pedagogy

By the end of this chapter you will be able to:

- identify the factors that influence pedagogy, particularly that associated with the use of technologies;
- understand the value of technology in supporting critical, creative and lateral thinking;
- appreciate the value of games and associated activities;
- describe the affordances associated with virtual learning environments; and
- describe the affordances of virtual worlds.

There are three pedagogies: that is, there is the traditional pedagogy of the classroom, there is the pedagogy for the adult, called 'andragogy', and there is the pedagogy of virtual worlds called 'cybergogy'. In this series of books on psychology for the classroom, this chapter usually reflects upon pedagogy with some important references to andragogy. However, this chapter focuses upon pedagogy as it relates to technology-enabled teaching and cybergogy as it relates to learning in virtual worlds. The first part of the chapter identifies and describes the key factors relating to the success of technology in teaching: belief, motivation, immediacy and different aspects of engagement. The virtual learning environment (VLE) is a key feature of teaching with technology and has an important role in pedagogy. The second part identifies the affordances and challenges to teaching of the VLE, including the routes of communication, social interactivity, engagement and assessment. Finally, an analysis of cybergogy in the virtual world is presented.

Using learning technologies

Pedagogy arises from considering theories related to learning and developing models for teaching. Pedagogy also arises through practice; the methods of and approaches to teaching develop through the processes of trial and improvement, practice and reflection. Figure 4.1 identifies the important factors that impact upon pedagogy and what we see happening in the classroom and in technology-enabled teaching.

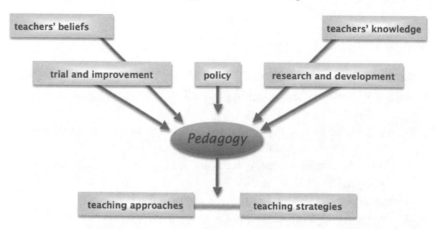

Figure 4.1 Pedagogy arising through theory, policy (politics) and practice

In traditional classrooms, the pedagogy underpins the strategies adopted by teachers. The nature of the classroom environment, the activities, the resources for learning and the regulation of activities and learning, all reflect the underpinning pedagogy. Mortimer (1999) describes the different ways in which pedagogy has been viewed in the recent past: types of teacher and styles of teaching; the teaching environment and contexts for teaching; teaching and learning as a collaboration between teacher and learner; and a policy/stakeholder view of teaching. In the recent past, the development of pedagogy with ICT has been both blighted and stimulated by the continual change that both technology and politics impose on teaching. That outside involvement, in both *how* teachers teach and *what* teachers teach, stems to a large extent from the UK Education Reform Act 1988 (OPSI, 1988), which dictates the curriculum. It gives a rationale for observing and measuring practice through agencies such as local education authorities, curriculum and assessment councils and the Office for Standards in Education (Ofsted).

Gráinne Conole and co-writers postulate the concept of the micro dimensions of e-learning. They identify areas of technology-enabled teaching and learning that include the organisational, technical, pedagogical and socio-cultural aspects including: interdisciplinary, access and inclusion, change, commodification, interactivity and social interaction and political aspects. The pedagogical aspects they identify include understanding and developing the:

- skills of teachers;
- skills of students;
- nature of online communities;
- different forms of communication;
- different forms of collaboration;
- modularisation, flexibility and interactivity;
- use of mobile learning (Conole and Oliver, 2007: 8).

When we consider technology-enabled learning, the technology artefacts tend to dominate the experience of the learners. The technology impacts upon the learning environment, the types of activities undertaken and the resources that may be used. The technology frequently, takes from the teacher and learner the regulation of learning. Bringing the focus away from the technology and towards the theories, Terry Mayes and Sara de Freitas describe the pedagogy of technology in terms of three broad perspectives: associative, cognitive and situative (Mayes and de Freitas, 2007). Their analysis can be simplistically interpreted as arising from the principles of behaviourism, cognitivism and social constructivism but, as stated in the introduction to this book, there are many more theories underpinning technology-enabled teaching and learning and the resulting pedagogies.

It is important to ask why some teachers adopt the use of computers in the classroom so enthusiastically and why that enthusiasm continues despite the constantly and rapidly changing frailties of technology and the challenges and difficulties associated with using computers in the class-room. The early adopters (Rogers, 1983) were 'seeing' the affordances (Kennewell, 2001) of the technology and balanced the cost/benefit positively, whilst others, described as laggards 'suspicious of change' (Rogers, 1983: 250), took a more negative stance and some were assertively negative (Luddites). In the early 1980s, several key reasons were identified for the efficacy of computers in the classroom. They included the motivational effect of the 'new' technologies, the non-judgemental nature of computer feedback and the immediacy of response of the computer. These factors continue to be important in the use of technology in teaching.

To a large extent, those generic reasons remain key to the continuing success of technology-enabled teaching. Avril Loveless reflects that 'technology doesn't change pedagogy – people do' but also states that the increased use of technology in teaching is causing educationalists to rethink their models of pedagogy (Loveless *et al.*, 2001: 63). She proposes that the teachers' influence and use of technology relate to their:

■ approaches to teaching;
■ beliefs about the subject matter;
■ subject knowledge;
■ pedagogic content knowledge;
■ craft skills in organisation and management;
■ personal characteristics and perceptions of the current situation;
■ teaching behaviours; and
■ context in which they are teaching (Loveless *et al.*, 2001: 68).

Belief

In the introduction to her book *Children Using Computers*, Anita Straker reflects on the pervasive nature of IT in society and the implications for teaching. 'Whether we like it or not, it is here to stay' (Straker, 1989: 2). In the late 1980s, there were two sorts of advocates of computing – those teachers who saw the new technology and said 'how can we use this in our teaching' and those who would say 'we have a challenge in our teaching – is it possible to use a computer to meet that challenge?' Those teacher beliefs have strong influences over the developments in ICT for teaching and learning; Rosie Turner-Bisset describes it as follows,

> Beliefs about a subject are informed by one's knowledge of substantive and syntactic structures of the subject. The same is true in education and teaching. If one believes education to be training, this belief shapes one's thinking, discourse and actions within education. (Turner-Bisset, 2001: 10–11)

The first way of thinking, assuming that the technology should be used because it is there, results in many innovative practices being tried and, perhaps, later discarded because they did not result in good and sustainable practice. For example, the laser disc mass-data storage technology of the late 1980s enabled the distribution of the Domesday Project which celebrated the 900th anniversary of the Domesday Book (1086) and contained thousands of photographs, articles and maps of Great Britain in a searchable and graphical format, running through the classroom computer. 'The BBC

Domesday project is a high profile example of "digital obsolescence" where technology has changed to the point that this once prestigious project has essentially disappeared less than a quarter of a century after it was completed' (Grant, 2009). The initial, obvious affordances of the system were soon rejected due to the difficulties of access experienced.

The second way of thinking – 'we have a challenge in our teaching' – created successful case studies and exemplars of practice. When scalable, the initiative enabled the wider use of ICT in teaching and learning. However, what works as an idea for a teacher or small group of teachers, may not work for everyone. This way of thinking also prompted the development of software applications and methods of working which proved unsustainable. There are two common teacher-beliefs. One belief is when they see the imaginative application of new technologies as a valid way forward because they are new. Another belief is that they only consider the use of an ICT initiative if they feel that it meets a pre-identified need. Teacher-beliefs are strong influences in the adoption of ICT in teaching and learning.

Motivation

Computers were seen to be motivating. 'Anyone who has watched children working with a computer is impressed by the increase in their motivation and concentration' (Straker, 1989: 3). This is in stark contrast to the observations that children have lost the power of concentration as a result of their continuous use of computer-based technology. There is no doubt that computer-based activities can be engaging to a level that is compulsive, exclusive, dominating and health-threatening. This aspect of computers and the engagement with the processing and screen imagery affects not only the game enthusiasts, but also those involved with social networking and those involved with programming.

In the 1980s, the motivational impact of computers related, to a large extent, to newness of the moment, termed the 'white heat of technology'. Computers were special and therefore seen by pupils as being worth 'doing'. Many pupils associated computers with games like the newly emerging Space Invaders and Pong which combined a narrative, such as stop the invaders or play an opponent, with quickness of reaction and finesse of hand. These genres were easily adopted by educational software developers to add competition, quickness of reaction or game rewards to the teaching elements, such as spelling, mental arithmetic or knowledge questions.

Computers were seen to be non-judgemental. Pupils did not seem to react badly to the computer when it corrected their mistakes – it was not personal. There seemed to be an acceptance of the decision and a motivation to get it right the next time. The 'punishment' for getting it wrong, withdrawal of the reward or a negative image such as a sad face, was accepted by the pupil. Even when the 'punishment' was a rewarding loud sound (raspberry) or appealing animation, there appeared an endeavour to get it right next time. 'Online assessment tests can provide immediate feedback in a non-judgemental way' (JISC, 2004: 26). Terry Freedman commented on the role of ICT in the light of the Every Child Matters agenda, 'teachers take advantage of the non-judgemental character of ICT to help children develop higher self-esteem' (Freedman, 2005: 15).

Emotional engagement

In 1986, my nephew came around to play with my children on our newly acquired BBC Master computer; we had a new game called *Granny's Garden*.

Granny's Garden by 4Mation was developed as an educational adventure game or microworld in which the user had to find six missing children (Esther, Tom, Anna, Jessica, Clare and Daniel), rescue them from the clutches of the Wicked Witch and return them to the King and Queen of the Mountains. There were logical puzzles and some guesswork – one wrong step in the forest and the witch would get you; with an eerie tune you were sent back to the start. *Granny's Garden* remains a firm favourite with teachers and children alike. Over the years it has obtained 'classic' status and is considered by many to be the definitive educational software problem-solving adventure for young children. The program has been updated to include a SCORM version for use in VLEs and remains as educationally useful as ever (4Mation, 2010).

The narrative of the story began, 'You are trying . . .'; it was 'you' who was trying to find the lost children; it was 'you' who the wicked witch would, perhaps, catch. After ten minutes or so of quiet play there was a sudden scream and then many tears from my nephew. The witch had caught him. In today's language we would say, 'the immersive nature of the simulation engaged both the physical and the emotional senses'. This is an early example of the computer's ability to represent a world and the user's existence in that world in such a way that the virtual experience becomes as real (in terms of perceptions) as the real world. If it had been termed 'e-safety' in 1986, then e-safety would have related to teachers' responsibility to present stories to children so that they are inspired and excited but not worried or frightened. Teachers would be required to consider the social and emotional aspects of learning.

Immediacy

As discussed above, many pupils were attracted by the interactive nature of the games and educational software. Simply the speed and the challenge to respond quickly, more quickly than their opponents or more quickly than the computer appeared to react, may have provided the motivation to complete the activities. The computer had a high degree of patience and did not become frustrated by delays in answering questions – the learner was in control of the pace of learning rather than the teacher. The relevance and the timeliness of the feedback provided a pedagogically sound teaching method; pupils know immediately if they are right or wrong because the computer provides a strong reinforcement of appropriate behaviour. In the speed-response and accuracy-response educational games there are strong connections with behaviourist approaches to learning. Keywords drawn directly from behaviourism and related directly to computer assisted learning activities include: observable behaviours, social environments, experiences, motivation, stimulus-response, conditioning, behaviour modification, modelling, rewards, punishments and affective domain.

More recent reflections on the reasons why computer enabled teaching can be effective are drawn from the JISC report *Effective Practice with e-Learning: A good practice guide in designing for learning*. It identifies key benefits that directly parallel those of a generation previously. The report reiterates learner control in 'self-paced' learning, the motivation effect of the graphics using the term 'media-rich resources', the value of quizzes and formative assessment through 'self-test', the immediacy of the interaction with 'immediate feedback' and the 'non-judgemental way' that computers communicate attainment and errors to the learner.

Online resources can support different learning styles and provide self-paced learning. Media-rich resources in different formats can provide more efficient learning when linked to face-to-face sessions in a blended learning programme. Online quizzes give learners opportunities to self-test prior to summative assessment. Online assessment tests can provide immediate feedback in a non-judgemental way. Individual learners can be more easily supported through differentiated resources (JISC, 2004: 26).

73

Action engagement

There is an uneasy relationship between games and learning. On the one hand, there is a celebration of the game/play values to learning. On the other hand, a distance is placed between the play/entertainment elements and learning by using the term 'serious' as in 'serious games'. However, it is plain to see that games engage the player, games engage the learner and engagement is a good measure of learning potential.

Marc Prensky identified 12 ways in which games appeal (Prensky, 2001c). Games give us enjoyment and pleasure (fun) through intense and passionate involvement (play). There is structure (rules), motivation (goals/win states), activity and outcomes. The latter, outcomes, Prensky relates to feedback and learning. Games are adaptive, require problem solving, promote interaction and develop emotion through narrative. Some computer games are long and complicated but still engage because of the higher level elements of motivation, emotion, interaction and interactivity. The features of computer games that encourage people to engage relate directly to those of cognition and learning (Gee, 2003). Game-based learning is the result of combining the 'game' characteristics with the learning 'context' or 'curriculum'. The model proposed by Rosemary Garris and colleagues adopts an 'Input Process Outcome' sequence (Garris *et al.*, 2002). First, it is proposed that an educational game is designed by integrating the teaching content with the game's characteristics. Second, the game program creates a learning cycle in which learners exercise their judgement and perform; meanwhile, the system provides feedback to learners. Good educational games, like good teaching, should give evaluation and feedback to improve the learners' study.

> Identifying significant mediating variables is an important step in under-standing the attraction of games and the effectiveness of instruction. Analyses of training effectiveness have revealed a number of variables that mediate training outcomes. Three such attitudinal constructs are locus of control, self-efficacy and valence. (Garris *et al.*, 2002: 13)

The locus of control is the willingness or ability of participants to engage in the process; the self-efficacy determines what activities the user will pursue, the effort they will make and the persistence they have to overcome the challenges; the valence is the attractiveness of the outcomes.

When learners engage in this cycle they are motivated to succeed. That success is achieving the goals, rewards and recognition of the game or achieving the learning outcomes. A fully educational game is when game outcome and the learning outcome are one and the same. Good educational games have to construct a cycle which motivates learners to learn continuously – they are learning in a highly contextualised environment and this form of learning relates to the situated learning theory (Brown *et al.*, 1989; Bruner, 1990; Lave and Wenger, 1991; Jarvis, 2004).

Cognitive engagement

A very early consideration of the impact of audio-visual resources on learning is that of Edgar Dale, who proposed a hierarchy of engagement in the learning process from the least engaging, reading about something, to the most engaging, actually carrying out the task by doing the real thing. His ideas present a realistic challenge to teachers and designers of technology-enabled learning experiences and can be used as a touchstone regarding pedagogic value.

---

reading
hearing *words*
looking at *pictures*
watching a moving image
looking at an *exhibit* of the artefact
watching a *demonstration* of the activity
seeing the *activity* being carried out on location
seeing and *discussing* the activity with other learners
preparing and giving a *spoken presentation* about the activity
preparing and then carrying out a *dramatic representation* of the activity
preparing, rehearsing and then *simulating* the real experience of the activity
doing the real thing

Source: Based on Dale (1969).

Figure 4.2 Hierarchy of engagement

When software-driven tasks are designed to present information in a predetermined, prestructured and didactic way, they lead to efficient knowledge transfer. When those tasks enable learners' achievements to be presented and assessed, then they lead to effective learning through feedback. When those tasks are drill and practice, they heighten response and accuracy and lead to more skilled learners. When the tasks enable collaboration and communication they lead to socially constructed learning that is both engaged and secure.

In contrast, when learners use software that engages them in critical thinking about what they know then they are using mindtools. Mindtools are at the heart of Papert's ideas when he proclaimed that computers would transform education. Mindtools are computer applications that engage the learner in analysing the information, they scaffold different forms of reasoning; they make learners think about what they are learning.

An important aspect of using a computer in this way is programming. When programming, the learners have to convert their ideas into computer formats. It is that intellectual process that:

- engages the learner with the material;
- requires them to analyse the material; and
- requires them to represent it in another format, usually as a sequence of events or a set of rules.

Programming is an important way in which the computer enables this process of engagement, analysis, transformation and representation. But programming is not the only way in which computers can support this form of learning. They can facilitate the learner in representing their ideas and understanding as visual representations (such as concept mapping), manipulating virtual environments (such as game authoring), causing actions (through avatar control). Papert's ideas have developed a flavour of constructivism called 'constructionism'. The theoretical basis of constructivism is that knowledge is built by the learner and not supplied by the teacher; the learner is actively engaged in interpreting and analysing. In social constructivism there is negotiation of meaning to develop common understandings. In constructionism, the understanding is derived from the learners' construction of new devices, ideas, knowledge, representations and sharing those with others. Mindtools facilitate that knowledge construction.

Mindtools do not simply enable construction; mindtools support engaged, critical, constructive and reflective thinking. Although the terms are frequently used interchangeably, it is useful to differentiate between those thinking activities that analyse with a degree of criticality, those that lead to new ideas and those that reflect upon or evaluate.

Mindtools are resources that support learning and have three important features:

1 they can represent knowledge, relationships or systems;
2 they are generalisable to different topic, theme, subject or curriculum areas; and
3 they foster some form of engagement through critical thinking.

Table 4.1 Analysis of critical thinking

Critical/Descriptive	Constructive/Creative	Reflective/Evaluative
measuring against criteria	sequencing and algorithm	drawing inferences
determining reliability	recognising patterns	identifying implications
recognising errors/ misconceptions	connecting – making links/ connections	deliberating/judging
abstracting	devising principles from experience/facts	prioritising
categorising	reorganising and representing	comparing/contrasting
testing hypotheses	representing in another form, finding alternatives	determining
identifying purpose	elaborating, developing, changing the purpose	usefulness/ appropriateness
	imagining, designing	relating to the personal
	inferring	relating to others

Table 4.2 Mindtools – functions and examples

	Represents knowledge	Represents relationships	Represents systems	Examples
word processor	✓			using a 'shared' document to develop a narrative; creating a template that can be used for many applications; changing styles to meet audience needs
spreadsheet	✓		✓	modelling real-life scenarios, such as theatre ticket sales or profit/loss scenarios
database manager (particularly relational databases)	✓	✓		identifying fields that represent, in the same structure, many disparate objects
presentation package	✓			sequencing or structuring knowledge to show understanding; using visualisations to represent the construct being presented
wiki, blog or forum	✓			presenting shared understanding; negotiating representations of knowledge; building knowledge through contributions
concept mapping software	✓	✓	✓	creating spider diagrams Mind Mapping™, Inspiration™, Kidspiration™
programming language			✓	LOGO, Scratch and Greenfoot
virtual world activities			✓	programming avatars (Kodu, 2010; Kar2ouche, 2010); designing environments (Habbo, 2010); adapting behaviours to other situations (Second Life®)

Creative and critical thinking

The competent and confident e-learner must have a degree of capability in handling information in the online environment. Edward de Bono wrote extensively about lateral thinking and the processes of generating novel solutions to problems. Although De Bono does not acknowledge any theoretical antecedents for his work on lateral thinking, it seems closely related to the Gestalt theory of Wertheimer, which founds its ideas of thinking and perception on a set of laws of organisation or grouping of ideas. Thinking and understanding are related to visualisation, including proximity, similarity, completeness (closure) and simplicity. For example, when trying to conceptualise ideas about e-learning the visualisations might include:

- the *proximity* of the relationship between asynchronicity/synchronicity with the cognitive/constructivist views of learning as reflected in Figure 2.1;
- the *similarity* between the personality and behaviours of an avatar and the personalities and behaviours of 'real' human beings;
- the *complete* dimension of the evaluation of e-resources is represented by the six areas of changing behaviour, constructing understanding, social construction, changing attitudes, developing maturity and satisfaction/ behaviour – see Figure 1.5;
- the *simplicity* of structures, such as the brain diagram to represent the interrelationship between Id and Ego in the Freudian interpretation of personality – see Figure 3.6.

Edward de Bono observed that 'western thinking' is concerned with analysis, judgement and argument. He contests that 'there is another whole aspect of thinking that is concerned with "what can be", which involves constructive thinking, creative thinking and "designing a way forward"' (de Bono, 1985: 2). His work has influenced the education of young children through, for example, *Six Thinking Hats*.

For older e-learners de Bono has identified four critical factors associated with lateral thinking:

1 recognising the dominant ideas that polarise perception of problems/ situations;
2 searching for different ways of looking at problems/situations;
3 relaxing the rigid control of thinking; and
4 the use of chance to encourage other ideas.

The primary school e-learner can benefit from being encouraged to think about the thinking strategies.

Table 4.3 The Six Hats and e-learning skills

Using the Six Hats	makes the learner consider...	and tutors/trainers/teachers are	resulting in...
The White Hat – Facts and information	what information is available and what is needed	ensuring learners have the Boolean skills of AND, OR and NOT and the understanding of keywords; controlling the range of data available (for example, a walled garden or permitted list)	effective and efficient users of technology
The Red Hat – Feelings and emotions	use intuition, feelings, and hunches	encourage learners to try not to be afraid, ensure they have the knowledge to back track (Control Z, browser back/ forward buttons, breadcrumbs and history)	confident and sensitive users of technology
The Black Hat – Critical judgement	be cautious and prepared for difficulties; be aware that things might go wrong	caution learners on e-safety rules and staying-safe strategies; but develop pupil resilience to inappropriate material and actions (Byron, 2008)	confident and resilient users of technology
The Yellow Hat – Positive values	identify values and benefits; identify why something might work	making the learners aware of functionality and affordances – what the systems can do and what the systems enable us to do	competent users of technology
The Green Hat – New ideas	generate alternatives and creative ideas	being imaginative with keywords when searching; exploring software and functionality; applying functions to resolve logic/data problems	imaginative users of technology
The Blue Hat – The big picture	manage the thinking process	using technology as a natural part of the teaching and learning process	
becoming the: competent, confident, effective, efficient, imaginative, resilient and sensitive e-learner.			

Source: Based on de Bono (1985).

The competent and confident e-learner adopts the appropriate strategy according to the situation being encountered. The provisionality of online environments continually presents the learner with novel and challenging visuals and opportunities and, to be competent, the e-learner has to possess strategies to deal with them. Lateral thinking offers important strategies. At the highest level, the e-learner makes decisions driven by strategies based on secure knowledge, driven by ambition and will, based on appropriate caution and care, using imagination and creativity within an overall strategic plan. The beginner e-learner needs guidance and tuition in the strategies. For the teacher, the first stage is to use the six hats, each in isolation – creating learning situations that are best tackled by the target 'hat'. Lateral thinking and the release of imagination to solve problems are important elements in creativity (Wickens, 2007), prediction and the application of interpolation and extrapolation (Woollard, 2007b). Aspects of lateral thinking that are useful strategies for pupils to adopt include being able to:

- develop concepts to breed new ideas and sharpen or change focus to improve creative efforts;
- break free from the limits of accepted ways of operating by challenging conventions and mores;
- use unconnected ideas and introduce elements of randomness to open new lines of thinking;
- harness the energy of provocation and move the thinking to constructive and useful ideas;
- select the best of early ideas and shape them into useable approaches and, in particular, apply those ideas to new situations.

Edward de Bono's book *The Five-day Course in Thinking* (1969) provides a good opportunity to show how computers can enhance learning. The problems, particularly the blocks examples, require the learner to physically or mentally manipulate blocks into different positions to meet particular conditions. By using a computer screen and mouse, the exercises can be completed by manipulating simple diagrams. The T-junction solution (de Bono, 1967: 103) is one that comes much more easily (for some people) when 'physically' manipulating the images (within the virtual environment of the computer screen) than trying to follow the process with mental imagery (in the head).

In contrast, his book *How to Have Creative Ideas* (de Bono, 2007) is not suitable for computerisation. In essence, the exercises are based on the use of randomly selected words with the learner imaginatively identifying connections and contrasts between individual words and groups of words.

The answers are based on semiotic, word shape and phonic characteristics of the words. An answer's correctness may depend on the history, context or feelings of the respondent and so be correct for him or her but not correct for anyone else. 'The fact that there are no right answers does NOT mean that any answer will do. The answer must satisfy the requirements of the exercise' (de Bono, 2007: 12). This is particularly challenging for conventional computer programming. It can deal with very fast responses to 'does the response match one of the correct answers?' It requires complex programming or time-consuming design to cater for many correct answers.

In conclusion, Edward de Bono's ideas on lateral thinking provide important guidance for supporting the e-learner in developing skills and aptitudes to handle the technology-enabled learning process. His ideas can provide the basis for some computer-based activities, but the nature of lateral thinking often generates many right answers that are difficult to codify within a fixed-state computer program.

Using virtual learning environments

The VLE is the dominant domain of technology-enabled learning for the start of the millennium. The decade has seen the progress from the first introductions of VLEs right through to the legislative requirement for all UK schools to adopt a VLE. The VLE is an important conceptual and theoretical paradigm to be understood. For the e-learner the VLE is as important as the classroom is for the traditional learner in school. The VLE embraces the technologies of Web 2.0 and presents them in a unified way within the protection of a secure, closed location.

The use of VLEs has become ubiquitous in UK education from the youngest entering school to the oldest leaving university. In infant schools, teachers are using VLEs, such as the Hampshire Wizkid to offer 'another style of learning (e-learning) which our pupils will meet later in their education ... [which] sits alongside traditional classroom teaching methods giving an opportunity to children who enjoy learning this way' (Freegrounds, 2010). Teachers can make available resources for the children to use in school, at the local library and at home. The systems have the full range of online resources including 'messaging facilities similar to email, chat areas and forums for discussion [where pupils] can develop their skills in this safe and closed environment with just their teachers and other pupils' (Freegrounds, 2010). The systems offer continuity between primary and secondary education. In some primary schools, the systems are used as a communication channel with parents. Secondary schools use them to regulate learning, both in the classroom, by being the source of learning objectives, teaching materials and assessment, and when pupils are working outside the classroom, prescribing homework, enabling the submission of homework, online tests for formative assessment and communication between pupil and teacher. In higher and further education they are used to 'manage' the education provision; the gateway to all courses is through the VLE. It is the standard method of distributing course information, teaching and learning resources, calendar and event information; it is focus for self-assessment and summative assessment activities and the route by which reporting of student performance is made. The VLE is having a dramatic impact on the learners' experiences, the strategies adopted by teachers and the development of the underlying pedagogy.

An early analysis of the use of a VLE to support learning adopted Mayes's conceptual framework (Mayes and Fowler, 1999) to describe the learning cycle which passes through the three aspects of conceptualisation, construction and dialogue. At the conceptualisation stage, the learner is exposed to new ideas or concepts through online experiences – those experiences involve orientation, exploration and experimentation. The construction stage involves the learner applying the new understanding/concepts in meaningful tasks, including selecting, linking and classifying material. The third stage, dialogue, involves the learner communicating their knowledge and understanding to others through discussion, reflection and reification – it is here that feedback from teachers and peers takes place and misconceptions may be identified. Michael Gardner describes the fundamental facilities of a generic learning platform and identifies that utilising a commercial product is attractive because 'it could provide a single service platform which could be used to provide tailored services to different market sectors [learners]' (Gardner and Ward, 1999: 19). The architecture is described in technology terms; this is reflected in psychology/learning terms in Table 4.4.

Online, distance-learning approaches cannot be successful without the learners having easy access to the full structure and resources of the learning programme. Although this can be achieved by providing open access to all the resources through the world wide web (for example, the teacher training programme for ICT teachers at the University of Southampton – http://www.pgce.soton.ac.uk/IT), many provisions require a degree of protection of resources and monitoring of access. The affordances of VLEs best meet those needs.

The nature of knowledge in the technology-enabled learning environment is changing. As a consequence, the way in which learners both perceive and acquire knowledge is also changing. The textbook was the

Table 4.4 Learning platform architecture and learning processes

Technology	Psychology
description of roles, personal information about learners/tutors	identifying of self, security, personal well-being
virtual classroom/meeting place, audio conferencing	starting to build a sense of community
private information spaces, file stores, the cloud	protecting the learner in the sensitive aspects of learning personal well-being
shared diary	ensuring online synchronous collaboration, social constructivism
modular coursework access, check points	structuring learning, supporting learning, regulating learning, feedback
email and discussion forum	asynchronous learning, representing understanding
spreadsheets, concept mapping, presentation software	mind tools for cognitivist activities
personalised home pages	raising esteem and developing personal well-being

Source: Based on Gardner and Ward (1999).

very life-blood of education up until the late 1990. 'The textbooks have been terminated by Arnold Schwarzenegger, the bodybuilding state governor who says they are "outdated" and too expensive' (*Times Online*, 2009). The VLE is proving to be the computer-based equivalent.

It is the design models for the VLEs that now underpin the teachers' strategies. The following list is based upon and extended from the work of John Cook and his analysis of the design of learning technologies (Cook *et al.*, 2006: 55). It is important that the teaching intentions are well-matched to the learning technology employed. In the examples presented in Table 4.5, the nature of the learning is matched to the affordances of the technologies. The third column reflects the typical impacts and changes that the introduction of technology has upon the learning environment. The statements do not avoid a focus on the negative and it is evident through considering the practices described below that there are positive and constructive impacts which make the introduction of technology-enabled learning a valid exercise. By focusing on the negative implications, the process can identify the areas where additional activity could be introduced to compensate for the perceived disadvantages.

Table 4.5 Teaching strategies and learning technologies

Nature of the learning	Learning technology	Characteristic impacts
Online, distance	VLE, MLE, WWW	the computer screen becomes *the sole medium* for learning; the tutor leads the learning by means of the technology – described by Laurillard (2002) as the narrative of her conversational model
Group and team work	social networks, asynchronous interaction through blogs, wikis and email, synchronous through internet messenger, chat rooms and CMC	the learner becomes an ID; they are represented *only by their words* – how they respond verbally in 1:1, many:many, 1:many and many:1 relationships
Assessment (summative/formative)	CAA, item banks, e-portfolios, patchwork	evidence becomes electronic; more immediate feedback; *less time to reflect* upon submission; feedback is *separated from* the learner–teacher relationship; assessment is *separated from* the learner–teacher relationship
Motivating and engaging	multimedia, virtual reality, game-play, virtual worlds	*disenfranchisement/ disadvantage* by those that do not 'buy into' the medium
Discovery and exploration	hypermedia, simulations, microworlds, game-play	*takes away* 'real' activity – reduces the kinaesthetic to finger movements
Personalisation	adaptive software, adaptive environments; portfolio systems	disenfranchises/devalues the teacher; *removes the physicality* of the product of learning
Informal, self-directed, open, independent, flexible	mobile learning, open-access WWW, ubiquitous computing	physically *isolates the learner* from other learners

Social interaction

Social interaction is a most important aspect of learning, regardless of the theoretical model that underpins the pedagogy: the behaviourist requires the interaction for the positive reinforcement and the social conditioning; for the social constructivist learning and understanding is the expression through language of that understanding; and the cognitivist sees the product of the thinking and thinking strategies through the interactions of the learner.

In the classroom, communication between teachers and pupils and between pupils and others is complex. A systematic analysis of the social interactions can be made (Edwards and Westgate, 1994; Kollias and Vosniadou, 2002; Bloome *et al.*, 2005). In technology-enabled environments similar analyses can be made (Martínez *et al.*, 2003; Mercer *et al.*, 2004). Figure 4.3 details the basic routes of communication; it can be used to illustrate and explain the functionality of the technology and the affordances that technology can bring to the teaching and learning process.

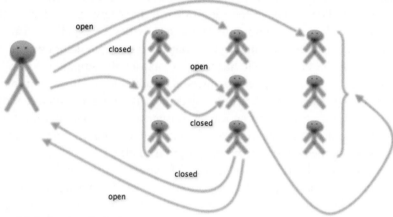

Figure 4.3 Routes of communication

An 'open' communication is one that can be seen/heard by everyone, for example, the teacher calling across the class or posting a message in a chat room. A closed communication is one where only the communicator and the recipient are aware of the message, for example, the teacher quietly telling a pupil to do something or the teacher sending a personal email. The teacher, tutor or trainer (on the left) communicates with the whole class/group, with individuals or with subgroups of the whole class. That communication can be open or closed. Superimposed on this diagram of the routes of communication are the labels of different types of communication. Ron Oliver and Catherine McLaughlin propose that there are five types of teacher–learner interaction: social, procedural, expository, explanatory and cognitive (Oliver and McLaughlin, 1996; Offir and Lev, 1999). The teacher will choose whether to employ open or closed or subgroup communication depending on the type of communication. This systematic approach will be used later to explain and describe technologies such as chat rooms, WIKIs and blogs.

Engagement

An important debate regarding the efficacy and efficiency of the learning systems is focussed upon 'quality' of provision. Tamer Abd El-Gawad's framework (Abd El-Gawad and Woollard, 2010) represents both the facilities and features of VLEs but also connects them with the stakeholders and their requirements of a VLE. The important educational psychology dimension of this quality model includes the flexibility of access and inter-activity to support associative (Mayes and de Freitas, 2007) teaching and learning, the range of social interaction opportunities (Web 2.0) to support social constructivism and the personalised learning to motivate and promote engagement. The challenge for educational technologists is to identify the affordances of VLEs and ensure the learning activities are experienced at the appropriate level of engagement. The following example demonstrates the principles of the engagement hierarchy. Consider the situation where an online experience is designed to introduce someone to simple computer programming. The lowest level of engagement is giving a written description of computer programming for the learner to read. The next levels are presenting still or moving images of computer programs. There is more engagement if the learner can see the program and the experience is particularly engaging if the program is in-situ. However, understanding how the program works may require the opportunity for the learner to express their developing knowledge and engage in socially constructed understanding. If the learner has to make a spoken presentation of the programming process they will be more engaged and more likely to understand or remember. If that demonstration were of the coding process in front of an audience, then the learner would be very engaged in the process.

However, there is a tension. In the practical situation there is often insufficient time for the learner to engage in the highest level of engagement for every topic. Also, it may generate a cognitive or emotional overload. The teacher needs to assess the appropriate level of engagement for a task based on the individual's needs, their previous experience, their capability and their potential to learn without very high levels of engagement. The skill of the teacher in combining their subject knowledge with the appropriate pedagogic approaches is known as pedagogic content knowledge (PCK) – a blend of content knowledge and pedagogic knowledge. Whereas content knowledge is a prerequisite for all communication about a subject, pedagogic knowledge serves as framework to scaffold the teachers' activities. In a similar way, pedagogic knowledge serves as the framework to scaffold technology-enabled learning activities. Educational technologists should be aware of the maxim, 'Those who can, do. Those who understand, teach' (Shulman, 1986: 14).

There is a further tension developing in schools. The 'work–life' balance is a well-known construct of adults. An important impact of the pervasive use of computers is that work, or aspects of the work, can so easily be taken home or, more correctly, accessed from home. The increased use of internet-accessible VLEs means that the learners' schoolwork is accessible from home. Homework is ceasing to be an add-on, preparation for the next lesson or follow-up from the previous. It can be exactly the same activity as is being pursued in the classroom. As teachers adopt more online activity whilst the learner is in class, the blurring of homework/classwork increases. The first signs of the learner's 'school–life' balance being impacted upon is the development of multiple GCSE programmes, such as Diplomas in Digital Applications (Edexcel, 2010), National Certificates (OCR, 2010) where four GCSE equivalent awards can be taught in the same number of lessons as two GCSE awards (10 per cent of the timetable). The time shortfall is addressed by learners doing more work, particularly on projects and skills development, outside of the school timetable and teachers doing more monitoring and assessments outside of the lessons. The role of the teacher may have to include providing information, advice and guidance raising 'work–life' balance issues.

Assessment

Assessment is an essential element of teaching. The VLE and technology-enabled teaching in general reflects the value of assessment; there are many aspects of the systems that contribute to the assessment process. Tables 4.6–4.8 identify the different aspects of assessment and describe the e-learning perspective connecting each with the significant learning theory.

Two aspects of assessment are currently in vogue, arising from the 'assessment for learning' initiatives (DfES, 2005; 2006; DCSF, 2008): peer-assessment and self-assessment. They tend to be episodic activities with structure and formalities.

The final classification of assessment types relates to the content of the quiz and how the results can be interpreted (Table 4.8).

The quiz is ubiquitous in computer-based assessments. Although the term suggests a degree of trivia, the sophistication and value of a particular quiz is determined by:

- the facilities of the system (question types);
- the degree of feedback to the learner and the tutor/teacher; and
- the skills of the author to construct a probe that gives useful information.

Table 4.6 Types of assessment: baseline, formative (diagnostic), ipsative and summative

	Description	Theory of learning	E-learning perspective
Baseline	before or at the start of learning to determine understanding, knowledge and skills – medium stakes, results determine teaching	behaviourist how do they respond? cognitivist what is their preferred learning style?	closed responses, no feedback, scores for different aspects of the curriculum/skills area
Formative (diagnostic)	during the learning process; identifies errors and misconceptions low stakes – learners may be unaware of the process; the process is seen to be supportive of learning; associated with feedback and assessment for learning	cognitivist how do they think? what are their preferred ways of learning? how do they represent their thinking? identifying errors and misconceptions	feedback to the tutor; similar to the baseline systems (ILS); some online and VLE-based quizzes send information to the tutor/teacher as well as the learner
Ipsative	measuring learners' attainment against their prior performance; low stakes when used in a formative mode; medium stakes when used to determine rewards, outcomes, future opportunities	behaviourist when used to reward and encourage constructivist when discussion of responses is undertaken cognitivist when errors and misconceptions are identified	only the adaptive systems and ILS can 'know' the learner and make judgements about current attainment compared with prior attainment
Summative	end of learning, measure of attainment in terms of mark/grade/level/performance statement, planned, structured, marked/graded/levelled and results reported – very high stakes, results have implications for future opportunities	behaviourist do they respond correctly? knowledge right/wrong do they respond quickly? skills are response rates sustained?	online tests, test centres, authentication of the respondent

Table 4.7 Peer-assessment and self-assessment

Peer-assessment	learners assessing each other's work; low stakes in terms of consequence but can be emotionally charged; usually not associated with summative assessment or baseline assessment	constructivist helping each other understand; coming to a shared understanding; cognitivist representation of understanding; identifying learning styles	peer assessment is a feature of current ICT teaching practice; ICT gives the opportunity for collaborative work; ICT gives the facility for whole-class presentation of an individual's work
Self-assessment	learners assessing own work; low stakes in terms of consequences when well-structured, supports assessment for learning; usually not associated with summative assessment or baseline assessment	constructivist representing understanding through oral and physical means; cognitivist representation of understanding; identifying learning styles	

Table 4.8 Forms of assessment

Criterion referenced	well-defined statements of success; tick box approach; the consequences determine whether this is high stakes or not	behaviourist responses meet the criteria or not; do they respond correctly?	
Norm referenced	results are usually numeric and can be compared to the results of a particular or the whole population – used for reading, spelling, non-verbal, quantitative assessments – IQ scores are norm referenced; typically used to determine grade, placements, potential therefore high stakes	behaviourist responses are right or wrong; to what degree do they respond correctly?	the quiz-like systems are used to deliver norm-referenced tests – these are only valid if taken under controlled conditions – authentication, test centres
Standardised	standards-based assessments are applied across populations but are not norm referenced; usually summative and therefore high stakes	behaviourist responses meet the criteria or not; do they respond correctly?	as with norm-referenced assessments above

Quizzes appear to be effective in the classroom because they engage the learners. There is a competitive element; there can be challenge; there is the opportunity for celebration and there is the opportunity for reward and positive reinforcement. In the classroom, there are other connected technology-enabled teaching devices that support interactivity, including tablet PCs (Gubacs-Collins and Juniu, 2009), the interactive whiteboard (Smith *et al.*, 2005; Kennewell *et al.*, 2008) and the classroom performance system (Wang *et al.*, 2009). In their own way, they each offer the same opportunities for competition, challenge, celebration and reward. It is through these devices that the teacher can gain very useful assessment data and also provide positive classroom experiences for the learners. The challenge is to enable quizzes in the VLE to engender and take advantage of those positive aspects as well as provide the teacher with useful data to help plan and provide appropriate learning experiences.

Cybergogy: learning in virtual worlds

Cybergogy is comprised of building learning archetypes to elicit responses from the four learning domains that classify the focus of sessions, the modes of teaching and the types of learning activity (Table 4.9). It is a pedagogy based on learning outcomes. The domains are:

- cognitive,
- dextrous,
- social, and
- emotional.

A teacher can plan to engage the learning domains to a greater or lesser degree, depending on the desired learning outcomes. However, by catering to all four domains, a learning experience can become compelling, holistic and immersive.

Within and across the learning domains are learning archetypes. They are the activities that learners carry out and they are the expectations of the tutors and teachers. They are the instructional strategies that act as the building blocks that facilitate learning. Learning archetypes (O'Driscoll, 2007), (Kapp and O'Driscoll, 2007) are pedagogic metaphors, a variety of activity types which can take a kinaesthetic approach comprised of concrete, physical actions, such as doing, being, moving and making, or a theoretical, conceptual approach composed of the cognitive processes of thinking, writing, describing and imagining (Woollard, 2004). Some archetypes can

Table 4.9 The learning domains of cybergogy

Domain	Description	Connections
Cognitive	Information processing (from remembering, recalling and archiving to analysing and critically evaluating) Application of knowledge in different contexts Creative intellectual activity; flexibility and plasticity of knowledge Hypothesis construction/destruction Retention of rules to abstract conjecture	Bloom's Taxonomy – cognitive domain Adapted by Anderson and Krathwohl (2001) Additional adaptation for Web 2.0 by Churches (2009)
Dextrous	Dexterity at the interface with the virtual world. Acquisition of skills for navigating, manipulating, inspecting and creating within the virtual world. Spatial awareness of depth and distance in three dimensions. Also required is dexterity with mouse, keyboard and other input devices and the ability to deal appropriately with personal items, in-world objects and communications across several modalities	With reference to Bloom's Taxonomy – psycho-motor domain
Social	Establishment of a sense of personal presence, awareness of the presence of others and understanding the context of interactions. Ability to relay and perceive meaning, particularly in text-based communications; to form affiliations and to network amongst them. Collaboration, co-creation and ability to discerningly filter and channel accurate information to identified groups or individuals	Adapted from Wang and Kang (2006) *Cybergogy for engaged learning*
Emotional	Perceiving emotional states of self and others and using emotional triggers to enhance learning experiences. The environment can provide emotional stimuli, including fear of falling, the visual of falling, excitement, tension and aesthetic appreciation. When learners are emotionally engaged, with each other in a spirit of camaraderie, the subject at hand, or the environment, a condition of immersion is attained which promotes deeper learning and retention. The nature of 3Di experiences means that it is suited to learning activities relating to personal, social, emotional and spiritual aspects of education	Salovey and Meyer (1994) 'Ability-based Model of Emotional Intelligence'; Goleman (1998) 'Working with Emotional Intelligence'; Zins et al. (2004) 'The scientific base linking social and emotional learning to school success'

display elements of combined metaphors, for example a theoretical metaphor such as thinking or creative imagining promotes and strengthens a resulting literal, kinaesthetic activity such as a persona dramatised in role play conducted within a 3D teaching and learning environment. The teaching design strategy that employs the integration of learning archetypes should take full advantage of the affordances of Second Life® such as the opportunity to provide synchronous experiences for learners who may be separated by great distance, allowing for interaction that feels very real, to provide a social networking opportunity promoting collaboration and the sharing of information and to create an alternative backdrop for learning that can break away from traditional settings and provide the opportunity for unique immersive experiential learning experiences.

Karl Kapp identifies a number of categories of learning archetypes (Kapp, 2007) including: role play, treasure hunts, guided tours, conceptual orienteering, operational application, co-creation, critical incident, group forum, small group work and social networking. This model is extended to include assessment adopting the structure of the REAP Model (JISC, 2007; REAP, 2007). The resulting structure has both frames and sub-frames associated with each archetype that exemplify appropriate teaching methods (Table 4.10).

The model is also extended to provide levels of implementation within each domain (Table 4.11).

The relation between domain, archetype, frame and sub-frame is illustrated in this example (Table 4.12). The 'Meshed' archetype is not simply the creation of opportunities to communicate but to creatively combine and interconnect individuals and groups in various ways for desired educational purposes and outcomes. In this example, the 'small group work' frame is selected – the teaching activity will relate to a nominated group working together on the activity and the major focus will be peer-to-peer communication and collaboration. At the lowest level of engagement the learner is making personal contributions. At a higher level they will be engaging with the group and becoming a member of the group through agreement, participation, consensus and mutual support (affiliation). At the highest level of working the learner will be acting as an intermediary for the group and representing the agreements of the group (channelling).

The final chapter contains two vignettes that relate to cybergogy. One describes the direct application of this theoretical approach in the development of a higher education curriculum. The second describes how activities to support teachers in training are developed in line with this pedagogy.

Table 4.10 The learning archetypes with frames and sub-frames

	Assessment	Meshed	Role play	Peregrination	Simulation
Frames and sub-frames	formative; summative; criterion-based; performance; reviews; e-Portfolios; learning contract, which might be: presentation multiple choice alternate choice short answer essay answer synergetic	co-creation; group forum; small group work; social networking, which might be: classroom emulation lecture demonstration presentation synchronous asynchronous mixed reality peer to peer	free form; structured; dramatised; morphic	treasure hunt; guided tour, which might be: escorted self-discovery adventure-based factual historical futuristic phantasmagorical morphic synergetic	conceptual; orienteering; operational; application; critical incident, which might be: physical interaction interpersonal interaction hybrid simulation blended (combining real world activities with virtual world activities) synergetic

Table 4.11 The levels of implementation for the domains of learning

Level of implementation	Cognitive domain	Emotional domain	Dextrous domain	Social domain
Level 1	Remembering	Perceiving emotion	Imitating	Personalising
Level 2	Understanding	Using emotion	Manipulating	Contextualising
Level 3	Applying	Understanding emotion	Developing precision	Communicating
Level 4	Analysing	Understanding emotions	Articulating	Affiliating
Level 5	Evaluating	Emotional self-control	Naturalising	Networking
Level 6	Creating	Influencing emotions	Authoritative	Channelling

Table 4.12 Exemplification of a learning activity within the social domain

Archetype	Frame	Sub-frame		Social domain
Meshed	Co-creation	Classroom emulation	1	**Personalising**
	Group forum	Lecture	2	**Contextualising**
		Demonstration	3	**Communicating**
	Small group work	Presentation	4	**Affiliating**
	Social networking	Synchronous	5	**Networking**
		Asynchronous	6	**Channelling**
		Mixed reality		
		Peer-to-peer		

Summary

Pedagogy is the theoretical basis of teaching. It is influenced by teachers' knowledge, teachers' beliefs, policy, research and reflection on practice. The pedagogic use of technology to enable and enhance teaching and learning is established through research and practice (see Figure 4.1). The degree to which teachers adopt the technology is influenced by the same factors as those influencing pedagogy as a whole. The impact areas of the use of technology include: motivation, emotional aspect, action and cognitive engagement, and creative and critical thinking. The influential technologies are: the internet-enabled VLE, internet and Web 2.0 technologies, subject-specific applications and the developing cybergogy of virtual worlds.

Activities

- Consider, in the light of the content of this chapter, the important aspects of the technology-enabled pedagogy and how they could be translated into teaching strategies.
- Consider the affordances of the virtual learning environment and establish a strategy for their full integration into a significant aspect of your teaching.
- Consider the affordances of virtual worlds and how they can support your work as a teacher.

5

Strategy

By the end of this chapter will be able to:

■ make informed choices about the appropriate application of technology within teaching and learning;
■ identify the underpinning theories of psychology and learning that determine pedagogy and teaching strategies;

and you will have:

■ reflected on the vignettes presented in the light of the preceding chapters and commentaries.

This section will outline some of the approaches taken by teachers who have discovered that technology can enhance teaching and learning, enable new activities to take place and increase opportunities for teaching and learning.

The characteristics of teaching with technology are:

■ providing ready access to the internet through networked computers, wireless and mobile devices;
■ using technologies that support and enhance the traditional craft skills of teachers of exposition, explanation, presentation and managing the activities of the learners;
■ enabling learners to access the curriculum, teaching activities and feedback when not in the classroom;
■ engaging in classroom conversations using technical terms in a confident and competent way;

- possessing a 'creative and constructively critical approach towards innovation, being prepared to adapt their practice where benefits and improvements are identified' (TDA, 2008).

Strategies of the technology-enabled teacher

A teacher who values the role of technologies will utilise all of the above approaches with the intention of assisting in the process of learning. They are based on the premise that technology can assist learning, technology-enabled teaching can be more efficient and effective and today's learners are responsive to technology. Bearing in mind that any individual teacher is likely to use a range of different approaches to encourage learning, the following approaches to organising learning activities in and beyond the classroom will be evident when a teacher has a bias towards directing learning through technology. Characteristics of teaching with technology include:

- integrating technology, such as interactive whiteboards, VLEs, class response systems, subject-specific software and internet-based resources, seamlessly into the classroom pedagogy;
- facilitating reward, reinforcement, stimulation and celebration (behaviourism);
- supporting communication with the learner, both in and out of the classroom (social constructivism);
- supporting learner communication with each other – leading to co-operation, collaboration and camaraderie (social constructivism);
- creating opportunities for socially-constructed representations of understanding, through wikis, forum and shared documents (social constructivism);
- encouraging learner autonomy and initiative through choosing when, how and what to learn;
- providing ways of exploring ideas and concepts; providing mindtools to aid presentation of ideas (cognitivism); and
- enabling control over systems through programming and scripting; developing understanding through quiz writing and presentations (constructionism).

Below is a series of vignettes set in classrooms or other learning contexts. Each of them illustrates at least one (and often more than one) of the situations in which a teacher has chosen to utilise technology in order to help the learners in each case achieve the learning outcomes set for the teaching. These vignettes are designed to ground the models, theories and principles of learning in the practices of current technology-enabled teaching.

Computer-mediated collaboration

In this example of technology-enabled learning in practice, the teachers are encouraging social interaction and dialogue between learners relating to e-safety issues using a conventional online chat room. The work is carried out making use of online websites related to e-safety and then using a computer-mediated dialogue via the medium of a closed chat room. The vignette illustrates a range of approaches to teaching that fall within the general area of supported social learning. It also illustrates that learners can operate in two media at the same time; they are creating presentations as well as simultaneously engaging in conversations within the chat environment.

The work took place with a group of mixed ability, mixed gender Year 7 pupils in a large urban secondary school. For one teacher it was a development of work associated with her continuing professional development. The activity was part of the Personal, Social and Health Education (PSHE) programme; learners were being given the

> opportunities to research, interpret and use a wide range of sources of information to inform their decision-making. This includes looking at the ways in which different media portray young people and health and social issues and present a balanced or partial view of issues. (QCDA, 2007: 250)

The National Curriculum continues, 'internet safety should be addressed explicitly'.

The traditional approach for the exercise is for pairs of pupils to independently create an e-safety presentation based on the teacher's presentation and exploring pre-assigned websites. The development of this idea superimposes the element of dialogue between pairs of pupils during the exploration, design and production phases of the activity. The teacher's exposition on e-safety was carried out during the preceding lesson.

The aim of the activity is to increase the learners' awareness of e-safety issues. The outcomes of the lesson, by which the learners' engagement can be measured, included:

- attentive listening to the presentation;
- on-task examination of websites;
- contribution to the online chat and the detail of the presentation produced.

The learners were individually subscribed to a private (bounded) chat room where only they and the teacher could read or write comments. The teacher, prior to the lesson, sent the first messages in the chat room. These initial messages described the activity and provided the URLs of the e-safety websites. The group entered the classroom, logged on and entered the chat room.

Where learners were uncertain about the process, they were able to check or ask within the chat environment. The teacher discouraged physical chat in the room so that the dialogues were all online. After experiencing several lessons with different groups, the teacher devised a set of rules relating to teacher online interventions:

- intervene through the chat room wherever possible;
- unless there is a health or safety or school discipline issue, never intervene physically;
- provide timed instructions through chat that are copy and pasted from a pre-written file;
- when appropriate, send positive statements (rewards, compliments, acknowledgements);
- when appropriate, send suggestions/ideas (modelling answers);
- encourage non-participants by asking them closed questions in the first instance; and
- guide off-task participants by asking them closed questions in the first instance.

Towards the end of the lesson the learners were encouraged to send copies of their e-safety rules, slogans or comments. In the final stages the teacher made plenary-like summary statements relating to e-safety.

Commentary

This vignette illustrates a range of approaches to teaching that fall within the realm of technology-enabled social learning. Dialogue mediated through technology, over large distances can be effective (Barak and Block, 2006; Bernard *et al.*, 2004; Danet *et al.*, 1995; Freiermuth and Jarrell, 2006; Grigsby, 2001; Kordaki, 2005; Richards, 2003). The key pedagogic features of the activity are:

- teacher regulation of learning;
- computer-mediated communication;
- differentiation by intervention (potential for strategic intervention);
- formative and informal assessment;

and some potential features are:

- peer assessment;
- celebration of learning;
- ICT skills development.

The teacher regulation in this vignette is strong. The learning outcomes are relatively fuzzy – being better aware of the issues of e–safety. The measure of whether learning has taken place is unlikely to be a post-experience test of facts. The measure is more likely to be an informal teacher assessment of learners' attitudes, along with some judgement of understanding based on the learners' responses during the activity. There is a need for strong teacher regulation of learning which takes the form of determining the topic area, controlling the pace, intervening if learners are off-task or not fully engaged and, finally, devising and delivering the plenary.

Computer-mediated communication is supported by social networking sites, virtual learning environments and a wide range of Web 2.0 technologies. In a later vignette, a 3Di environment is used to support learning through social interaction. As described previously (see Chapter 4, Figure 4.3), there are ten potential routes of discourse. The chat room form of computer-mediated communication does not provide 'closed' communication and the number of routes is therefore limited. They include:

- teacher to the whole chat room;
- teacher to an individual learner (but open – readable by all);
- learner to the whole chat room;
- learner to the teacher (but open – readable by all); and
- learner to individual co-learner (but open – readable by all).

The traditional classroom has all these forms of communication between teacher and learners and learners with each other and each serves its particular purpose in classroom management (managing the resources of learning), behaviour management and curriculum management (regulation of learning). There is a high degree of complexity of human–human communication by verbal and non-verbal means and 'closed' communication between individuals can take place without others being aware of the content. The sophistication of communication in the traditional classroom is high but in this basic chat room scenario, there is no potential for 'closed' communication between individuals.

Sustained online learning

This vignette describes a technology-enabled learning experience that delivers a complete three-year undergraduate BA (Honours) degree with no face-to-face element, called 'Learning Through Technology' through Ultraversity at Anglia Ruskin University. It is a part-time and distance learning programme with a typical online learning commitment of 15–20 hours per week. The programme is work-based with students using their day-to-day experiences as the context for their academic pursuit and assignment submissions. All teaching is delivered online and, like most traditional programmes, students are assigned personal tutors who oversee course content, progress and achievement. The online community of fellow students is an important element of the learning experience.

The features of this form of technology-enabled learning that are worthy of note are: the sustained nature of the learning, the high level of academic pursuit and the methods of evidencing attainment.

Sustained learning

For sustained learning to be successful there needs to be a high level of commitment on behalf of the learner and the appropriate structures in place to support that commitment. The structures are both of a physical nature (the online environment) and those of policy (the procedures and expectations of the system).

The programme is supported by a number of technologies, each designed for a particular purpose in the learning experience and they include commercial and open-source resources. For example, there is a Facebook presence and they use Google Docs for collaboration and communication. For the anonymised submission of work and its processing through the assessment, second marking and moderation processes they use the open source virtual learning environment Plone® (http://plone.org) running on the University's servers. They use the commercial product First Class® (http://www.firstclass.com) for communication both through email and by sharing documents. It is a 'single system' approach with the features and capabilities necessary to enable communication, collaboration and learning for the post-16 and higher education student. The tutors and students use mobile telephones and conference calls to communicate.

Personalisation is a strong feature of the underpinning policy. The policy is reflected in the nature of assignments and the way in which assignments are assessed. The assignments are reflected in the activities and the underlying core curriculum that focuses on:

- enabling students to take charge of their professional development and devising strategies to do that;
- developing skills of action inquiry situated in their working context;
- promoting capability to commit to lifelong learning;
- promoting a positive and flexible attitude to change;
- raising self-awareness and students' recognition of their abilities; and
- providing the knowledge and understanding to help the students influence change.

The students' commitment to sustained learning is promoted through these curriculum aims.

Academic pursuit

A high level of academic pursuit is a particular feature of this technology-enabled approach. To ensure that the learners can operate at undergraduate level mechanisms must in place that accommodate learning and assessment that are above the knowing and doing level of cognition, but can support the analysis, synthesis and evaluative levels (Bloom and Krathwohl, 1956). The students are required to:

- analyse and evaluate their learning experiences and requirements;
- research appropriate sources to gain knowledge and skills;

- develop, plan and implement projects; and
- communicate effectively at a range of levels within the workplace.

The challenge of technology-enabled teaching is to prevent the curriculum being dumbed down by the requirement to express every iota of the teaching in words on web pages. One solution is the assessment model, which is discussed below. The other is to make the learning environment and the activities 'situated' (Lave and Wenger, 1991), that is, embedded in the real world of the work-base context and the academic world of authoritative online resources. The students learn in learning communities based on the concept of a 'Community of Practice' (Wenger, 1998), where they have continual and required contact with peers and others operating at the high academic level.

Assessment method

The materials the students make available for assessment are placed in an e-portfolio. The model of presentation is based on Richard Winter's 'patchwork text' (Scoggins and Winter, 1999; Winter, 2003) where writing and resources develop throughout the module as small 'patches', which are then stitched together, typically with a reflective commentary. The overall effect is summarised by a single document that describes the issues and conclusions but also makes direct reference to the evidence. Patchwork text is the assembly and stitching of text and is described as a 'coming to know' or 'making sense over time' (Winter, 2003:120). The approach builds in the sharing of draft patches for peer formative feedback ('peer review'). A feature of patchwork writing is that it is continuingly developmental and never finished, similar to the perception of socially constructed understanding as an organic process that never ends as each person contributes their understanding to the collective.

Commentary

Technology-enabled learning is influential in the lives of those in education. This vignette describes a project that has implications for social justice. The course 'was based upon the premise that conventional models of study at university fail to meet the needs of a significant number of potential students and their employers' (Powell *et al.*, 2008: 63). Stephen Powell, in his analysis of the course, observes that for a significant group of students face-to-face attendance can be perceived as too expensive and has employment issues. The vignette also illustrates how technology can empower learners at a distance to engage in cooperative and collaborative work leading to socially-constructed understanding. The use of technology enables a wider use of media in the production of work for assessment and they have developed the model into 'Patchwork Media' (Arnold *et al.*, 2009). It should be noted that 'an increasing number of students report that they are making use of an iPhone Application version of FirstClass Client to access and communicate – in addition they are using internet-enabled handhelds generally to access the course'. The third important aspect of technology-enabled teaching is that it builds the capacity for sustained and lifelong learning. The technology accommodates 'Assessment for Learning' (Black and Wiliam, 1998a; 1998b) and indeed could be seen as 'Assessment as Learning' (Boud and Falchikov, 2005; Carless, 2007). This approach builds the student's capability for effective self-assessment, a vital component of lifelong learning and 'sustainable assessment' (Boud, 2000; Boud and Falchikov, 2005).

This approach to teaching, in which the learners have little or no face-to-face contact with the teacher, tutor or trainer, may become a regular feature in schools. It is reflected in the support we currently give to certain pupils for some of their courses.

Teaching in the virtual world

Drury University in Springfield, Missouri, USA is an independent university with a strong investment in online education. Traditionally, Drury's online courses are conducted using a learning management system (presently Blackboard) to deliver content. However, members of the Online Education directorship are interested in pioneering an opportunity to increase the immersive quality of distance courses for participants and to foster a sense of community spirit amongst geographically distributed learners by enhancing some courses with a 3D immersive Virtual World (3DiVW) component. Second Life® is the chosen delivery platform owing to its affordances in terms of accessibility, multi-modal communication facilities and advanced user content creation opportunities. In preparation for the shift to 3DiVW, Drury University's Online Education e-Tutors require professional development and guidelines in order to transition course materials and teaching strategies away from the familiar 2D computer mediated model of the learning management system towards a framework that supports the potential of the learning environment presented by Second Life®.

Every Tuesday morning at 11.00 am (CT) the Drury's e-tutors follow structured activities of professional development in training events conducted within the virtual world. This synchronous programme covers course design based on an understanding and application of the Cybergogy of Learning Archetypes. Introducing the e-tutors to cybergogy takes place in stages. Initially, the 'Efficacy Analysis Matrix' (EAM) is introduced as a pragmatic measure to assist e-tutors in evaluating discerningly the overall effectiveness of delivering content using Second Life®. Use of the EAM provides a preliminary opportunity for e-tutors to critically analyse the environment for implementation of specific learning activities in terms of three key aspects:

- conjectured effectiveness for learners – (is the use of Second Life gratuitous?)
- feasibility of implementation and management – (is the activity sustainable in the environment?) and viability of content quantity and quality – (can the learning activity produce the desired learning outcomes in a timely, economic manner?).

The objective is to encourage e-tutors to re-examine their syllabus under the lens of Second Life and to exploit opportunities which can enhance their teaching by providing a learning experience with a greater level of immersion than by other available means and to identify incidents where straightforward delivery by conventional VLE would be more effective, therefore minimising counter arguments that Second Life is being used frivolously or without substantiation. Then, the e-tutors identify the two interacting components: learning domains and learning archetypes. Learning domains are strands drawn from real world understanding of pedagogy and cover the four areas of cognitive, emotional, dextrous and social learning designed to draw forth all of a person's sensibilities into the virtual environment. The learning archetypes are the activities with which the learners' avatars engage when in the virtual world; they act as a vehicle towards attaining a condition of immersion. The e-tutors establish learning outcomes by identifying the learning domain and selecting the learning archetypes to best achieve the outcomes. Further details of the theory of cybergogy (pedagogy in the virtual world) are described in Chapter 4.

The Drury University e-tutors are developing learning activities, for example:

- *Role-plays* – Social Psychology instructor, Fenix Muhindra, introduces students to experimental gender exchange in Second Life. Students are required to remodel their avatars from female to male and vice versa and to role-play a transposed sexuality role reporting on their thoughts, feelings and experiences and on any interactions they encounter whilst in character.

- *Peregrination* – Arab Israeli Conflict Studies instructor, HG Vayander, takes students to sites in Second Life, such as The Western Wall (or Wailing Wall) where a prayer can be written and delivered from the virtual world to be placed in the crevices of the real wall in Jerusalem. Orthodox traditions extend from the real world into Second Life, women (female avatars) are not allowed to pray at the wall but are to remain behind a barrier at the location.

- *Simulations* – Astrology and Physics instructor, Orion Haystack, uses virtual telescopes to simulate the use of powerful real world telescopes to view images of star formations, asteroids, comets and such. Importantly, these are not web-based images; the learning experience is available purely from within the Drury island within Second Life.

- *Meshed* – the social constructivist aspect of the meshed archetype is employed during the orientation of Drury's Online Education students new to Second Life conducted by Samaj Susanowa. They are brought together by semester to network, collaborate and learn from each other. With the support of instructors they learn basic skills of dexterity by imitation to support their in-world learning activities. Students are encouraged to form affiliations, join groups and personalise their avatars. Communication skills (voice, instant messaging and local text-based chat) are honed during this time. Students experiment with adjusting their computer system settings to deliver an optimum virtual experience.

- *Assessment* – all instructors carry out formative and summative assessments virtually, using tools for surveys, presentations and assignment submissions.

Drury University's e-tutors final assessment requires them to participate in six hours of teaching practice within the virtual world as
virtual tutors (v-tutors). This consolidates their conceptual realign-
ment to the ways of teaching and learning in the virtual world. They
are immersed in the 3Di environment, the model of cybergogy and
the v-teaching practices. This maximises the potential of the tutors'
ability to 'splice teaching and learning away from classical methods of
online delivery of education and training' (Scopes, 2009: 19) to present learning opportunities that are unfettered by real life constraints.

Commentary

The social constructivist model of cybergogy of learning archetypes is identified as being the most pertinent, deriving philosophically from the
Vygotskian socio-cultural approach of knowledge internalisation supported
by social processes leading to the development of higher cognitive functions. Virtual world learning is enabled through the new pedagogy called
cybergogy. It enables the unique features of the virtual world to provide
immersive experiences that would otherwise be too expensive, dangerous,
remote or unimaginable using conventional pedagogy.

Using authoring to increase learner engagement

This vignette describes how learners can be more engaged with the knowledge associated with their learning by creating quizzes for others to
complete. In this particular scenario, the learners are Key Stage 2 pupils but
this strategy works easily well for older learners producing quizzes for peers,
younger people or another defined audience. The pupils use an online quiz
programme provided through the school's VLE. The activity promotes a
deeper knowledge and understanding of the topic of the quiz and creates a
focus for collaboration between pupils and a better understanding of the
subject matter.

The series of lessons relates to providing an overview of how British
society was shaped by the movement and settlement of different
peoples in the period before the Norman Conquest and an in-depth
study of how British society was affected by Roman or Anglo-Saxon
or Viking settlement. The teacher's planning includes the following
statement:

Introduce the pupils to the quiz writer in the VLE, demonstrate the entry of a single question and save to the 'sandpit'; explain that in the 'sandpit' their quiz can be looked at and changed by other pupils – do not look at someone else's nor make changes without their permission. Talk about the different sorts of questions and the best type to be used, giving examples. Break into pairs to plan quizzes on the assigned topic of 'Romans', ' Saxons' or 'Vikings'. Remember, the audience for your quiz are the other groups.

The National Curriculum for History at Key Stage 2 includes

Romans, Anglo-Saxons and Vikings in Britain.

Effects of Roman settlement: the Roman Conquest and occupation of Britain; Boudicca, Caratacus and resistance to Roman rule; the building of Hadrian's Wall, roads, villas and towns by the Romans; Roman settlement in the local area.

Effects of Anglo-Saxon settlement: the arrival and settlement of the Anglo-Saxons; the conversion to Christianity, the lives of monks and nuns, for example Bede and Hilda; religious beliefs and customs, including the Sutton Hoo and other ship burials, and myths and legends; Anglo-Saxon settlement in the local area.

Effects of Viking settlement: Viking raids and settlement; King Alfred and Anglo-Saxon resistance to the Vikings; King Cnut and the Danes; Jorvik and other Viking settlements; heroic poems and sagas; Viking settlement in the local area (QCA, 1999: 19).

These words are the starting points for the text and questions of the quizzes.

At the end of the activity the teacher has a number of quizzes – five on Romans, five on Saxons and four on Vikings. These are teaching resources for the future as well as the focus for the 'compare and contrast the historical developments' activities for the current group.

Commentary

The learning outcomes the teacher was aiming for were that pupils should

show factual knowledge and understanding of aspects of the history of Britain ... describe characteristic features of past societies and periods ...

identify changes within and across different periods ... describe some of the main events, people and changes ... give some reasons for, and results of, the main events and changes. (QCA, 1999: 39)

The classroom environment and limits on the access to computers did not permit extensive online research and compilation of information. If more computer time is available then the further attainments specified by the National Curriculum may be achieved – 'beginning to select and combine information from different sources ... produce structured work, making appropriate use of dates and terms' (QCA, 1999: 39).

The reaction of pupils to the writing of quizzes is mixed. They are motivated by the topics and would like to create a quiz but the quiz writing mechanism is rather complex and not particularly intuitive for the pupils. They do not necessarily have the same frustrations when authoring crosswords or quizzes by hand. Time is lost because some pupils find it difficult to grasp the value of the different question types. The outcomes for the successful are very good. They gain in three important ways:

1   they better understand the structure and mechanisms of quiz making and so have a mindtool for future use;
2   they can reflect their knowledge and understanding of the topic in a creative and rewarding way; and
3   they create a product that has real value for the class and the teacher.

The teachers' observations include the following:

■   it is important to explain the different question types, particularly the popular multi-choice and short-answer questions;
■   to add value to the activity pupils need to be encouraged to add text to the question to set it in a context (for example, the question, 'Who led the Britons against the Roman invasion?' is not as valuable as 'In 43 AD the Romans landed on the shores of Britain. They conquered many tribal groups but allowed the kings to rule their own areas. Some people were not treated well by the Romans and they revolted. Who led the Celts against the Romans during that time?');
■   pupils needed to be taught how to create plausible wrong answers for the multiple-choice questions (for example, the choices: Minnie Mouse, Dracula, Boudicca, Madonna and Jedward, are not as good as: Bede, Hilda, Boudicca, Caratacus and King Cnut);
■   the teacher must continually and rigorously check the authoring of the questions and answers to prevent pupils being exposed to others' errors and misconceptions.

It is that thinking which is critical to the value of authoring for understanding and the basis of the constructionist approach. An important feature of some quiz writing applications is the ability to allow the learner to 'mark their own work', enabling the quiz to become a teaching tool in the spirit of 'Assessment for Learning' (DfES, 2005; Black and Wiliam, 1998a; 1998b).

Feedback is an important aspect of all learning theories. The behaviourist approach suggests that being rewarded for obtaining the correct answer will reinforce the appropriate actions. The constructivist sees it as an essential aspect of knowing that the developing model is correct. The social constructivist will want the language dialogue extending beyond the learner-computer but within itself, that exchange is reinforcing of the learner's understanding. The quiz authoring itself is a constructionist activity and the software system is a mindtool supporting cognitive approaches.

The feedback from the quizzes in general takes several forms. The simplest is the pupils checking whether they have answered individual questions correctly or not. Sometimes a scoring system can award marks to individual questions, thus allowing harder questions to be weighted more than easier questions. The final score can indicate overall performance. That score can be automatically e-mailed to the learner completing the quiz or to the teacher. The most sophisticated feedback records log files tracking the performance of the individual on each separate question, the time taken to complete the activity and the name (identifier) of the computer used.

Professionals learning in the virtual world

This vignette focuses on the use of a virtual world in postgraduate teacher training. Features of the experience include the following:

- the physical location of the activity is the trainee's choice;
- elements of the activities are new to every participant;
- trainees have to adopt an avatar to represent themselves;
- activities develop skills relating to dexterity and peregrination.

There are challenges for teaching and learning in particular virtual world environments but these activities provide experiences that enhance trainee teachers' skills, knowledge and understanding of 3Di and technology-enhanced learning in general. This vignette comprises a small selection of the comments made by trainees following their first visit to Second Life®.

This first experience of a multiuser environment inspires some trainees:

> I created an avatar called 'Teaching ★★★★★★'. It was a valuable experience as I had not been to Second Life before ... I then made my way to the public sandbox along with other members of the PGCE. From there I tried to manipulate and build objects ... I feel that there is more potential in Second Life than I had originally perceived. I think it would useful as a long distance learning tool/environment. Because it is more stimulating than chat rooms or groups (good for students that need both visual and audio tools to learn), and it's more personal than instant messaging.

Others met technical difficulties or challenges with the interface:

> Second Life was interesting and whilst I was unable to navigate around the world, I did watch some of the interesting tutorials on the things that you could do whilst in the environment. This experience allowed me to gain an insight into why it is so hard to engage the pupils with ICT teaching, and maybe this sort of virtual world could be a way to engage them more.

> With instant message help, I succeeded in uploading my picture and adding it as a texture to a box primitive.

Participants were able to reflect upon the affordances and challenges of virtual world teaching.

> The major issue was finding the PGCE IT Staffroom and as a result, the other problem with exploring environments – it is easy to waste time!

> The positive aspects of the day were using new software such as Second Life, which has been extremely time consuming, but has shown me that, working collaboratively, I was able to grasp the basics and get on with the product. I can see that introducing a new piece of software in a classroom would need to be done in stages, with guidelines and help rather than making it a self-taught class. So pupils, like me, would get frustrated with the seemingly unhelpful screen in front of them.

There are a number of reported technical difficulties with the Second Life® application. The frequency and nature of those difficulties are significant and should be considered when planning a virtual world teaching session for the first time. Finally, a comment on the immersive nature of working in virtual worlds:

> For some reason I could not teleport and after much help from Light Sequent and John I still could not follow the others. I recall a moment when Light Sequent said to me 'Don't worry I wouldn't leave you alone', which made me giggle. How silly, I thought, 'its only Second Life'. Eventually Light Sequent did have to leave me alone due to her commitments to the group, and I can honestly say for a split second I actually did feel abandoned. Then after 10 minutes of waiting for teleportation I felt a little lonely. Feeling these emotions made me realise the full potential of building and maintaining relationships in Second Life. I felt the same frustration and disappointment about not being able to join the rest of the trainees as I would have if I had been locked out of or stopped from entering a room during a training session at University.
>
> This emotional response is an expression of 'immersion' with the environment. Personally, I view this as an extremely healthy experience, especially at such an early stage of adoption ... this example serves to demonstrate how easy it is to both project and perceive a personal presence in the virtual world ... this is a powerful tool for teachers indeed. (Woollard and Scopes, 2010: 4)

Commentary

The popularity of online gaming, the demonstrable value of interactive programs for teaching and training and the growing potential for teachers to design and build their own 3Di environments, makes an imperative that teacher training includes experience of virtual worlds such as Second Life® (http://secondlife.com). An online day where trainees work on their computers, in their work or home environment, offers many opportunities for them to be independent and personalise their own learning. As noted by Kristen Moore and Ehren Pflugfelder, there is a need for pedagogical and technological scaffolding in preparation for taking students into online environments if they are to function as 'fun and creative spaces' (Moore and Pflugfelder, 2010). The significant challenges are of a technical nature but the structure and resourcing for the online day must be considered so that individuals do not feel isolated or unsupported. Subsequent visits elicited an increase in positive impressions as the students began to feel less estranged in the virtual environment. The third and final Online Day is structured to give the students a choice of peregrination activities consisting of matched pairs of in world locations that present contrasting experiences. Trainees are asked to consider the locations in terms of the impact on each of the four learning domains discussed in the cybergogy sections, cognitive, emotional, dextrous and social.

PEREGRINATION PACKAGES

Science	Aesthetic
Health	Art
Historical	Fantasy

Figure 5.1 Three contrasting peregrination choices

Comments made by the trainee teachers following this activity:

'The Particle Accelerator activity was graphically impressive and probably a very good illustration for a pupil, however the accompanying text was much too high-level to be of any practical benefit. The graphics at this point, however, were some of the best seen so far in a virtual environment.'

'Overall this learning experience encountered problems, yet there is merit to it, as technology and internet speeds develop, I see this as a viable learning platform.'

'The potential to stimulate learning is immense.'

'It has a really WOW factor, with opportunities for gathering information that exceed real life.'

'I found this room intriguing, I assumed that this sort of set up could be used for video conferencing, amazing! This would be so much cheaper to set up and run than standard video conferencing suites for schools and so widen the opportunities for pupils.'

'It feels a bit strange walking around an environment where you don't actually know the social rules, and the social rules are definitely an area that needs to be defined in an online virtual environment when considering the mental and physical well-being of pupils.'

'This is my third visit to Second Life and whilst still a little unsure of how to do things, I feel confident in my ability to move around and manipulate the environment. I think that initially pupils would need some help with the interface; they would soon be comfortable with using it.'

'The Lost Gardens of Apollo was the first site I visited and is clearly the aesthetics-focussed site of the two packages. It was a very beautiful site and gave you a clear sense of visiting another, cohesive world.'

'In terms of how it lends itself to learning, if we start with how it may allow us to stretch our cognitive capabilities, a possible use for this kind of environment would be one of simple exploration.'

'The social and aesthetic quality of such a task would lend it to being an emotional experience. All of these learning threads should allow for improved learning and recall due to the multifaceted ways of encoding the learnt information through the rich experience.'

'I really enjoyed that environment [art]. Some of the pieces were lovely. In the Art environment I was pleased to learn how to jump and move forward so that I could scale a wall. I was surprised when I found I could fly and walk through windows.'

'The most striking exhibit I found to be the "hiding place", which oozed claustrophobic dread. The authentic photo was poignant.'

'Despite the occasional technological glitches, I am very positive about the affordances of SL for teaching and learning as a forum for tolerance, information and knowledge exchange, and a locus of practical creative learning, all of which can happen in a collaborative, engaging manner.'

'The holocaust museum was effective on a cognitive level. There was a lot of information on the notice boards that made you think. I found the fantasy environment very peaceful and calming.'

E-safety in learning and teaching

This vignette describes one school's initiative to raise the profile of e-safety with parents as well as give clear information, advice and guidance to pupils. In Glenwood School e-safety is coordinated by the ICT subject leader but involves the pastoral teams, the teacher responsible for child protection and sessions taking place in Personal, Social, Health and Citizenship Edication (PSHCE) as well as ICT lessons.

> 'E-safety is a whole school issue' was the opening remark; the head teacher goes on to explain the importance of the staff development day and the strategies that were being put in place to ensure the safety and well-being of pupils and staff with regard to the use of all forms of technology in teaching, administration and personal use.
>
> The training session was designed around Tanya Byron's analysis based on the 3'C's of pupil content, contact and conduct (see Table 5.1). Through small group discussions, individual tasks and whole staff plenaries, the school has developed a shared understanding of the issues of e-safety, the resources available, the procedures and policies in place. Most importantly, the session ensured that the teachers had confidence that they, as well as the pupils, will be supported if e-safety issues arise.

Commentary

It is noted that children online are less risk-averse in their dealings with others. 'Over 75 percent of Internet users feel safer speaking their mind when they use an avatar' (Meadows, 2008: 36). They feel safer and speak more readily with those that they do not know in the physical sense but only know in the virtual world. 'The lack of contextual clues frees up social inhibition but also loosens commitment and trust' (Shortis, 2001: 97). They more readily confide secrets and more readily expose themselves in both a physical way (Childnet, 2005) and in a verbal way. Mark Meadows describes the avatar as a tool for regulating intimacy because intimacy and interaction with others are more easily controlled. In real life it can be difficult to remove oneself physically from uncomfortable positions but in the virtual world 'isolation' or 'home' is always just a mouse click or key press away. But, as Mark Meadows explains,

> in a world where information is more important than physical proximity, we are not as safe as we might assume … I have seen some extreme tragedies unfold because of the assumption of the mask … because we can immerse ourselves more and more into these environments we let our guards down. (Meadows, 2008: 36)

Ringo Ma's study of student use of bulletin boards reveals that participants disclose personal information without acknowledging the consequences of that disclosure (Ma, 1996). The Byron Review in the UK identified an important element of education with regard to e-safety as developing children's hardiness in the face of inappropriate and potentially damaging materials and contacts that the internet presents. The report of the review states, 'we must also build children's resilience to the material to which they may be exposed so that they have the confidence and skills to navigate these new media waters more safely' (Byron, 2008: 8). In terms of the model presented by Freud, we need to ensure the motivations of the Id (repressed and modified through the Ego by social mores) determine that the learner behaves in a safe way. Freud's 'cap of hearing' is the key. We have to ensure that the learner has the opportunity to 'hear' clear and actionable information about their online lives. The 'hear' includes seeing appropriate behaviour by peers and models, experiencing appropriate scenarios, being rewarded for behaving appropriately as well as being given appropriate information, advice and guidance. The three 'C's of content, contact and conduct, that Byron proposes help guide the provision of information, advice and guidance to learners.

In Freud's world there is an important factor that modifies behaviour – it is the sex drive or libido. Freud's assertion is that repressed sexual drive leads to problems in later life. By articulating this explanation of human behaviour, Freud has been criticised for allowing some to excuse their behaviours and the behaviours of others rather than taking direct responsibility for their actions. The e-safety issue is brought into sharp focus because of the combined effect of:

■ younger users of the internet feeling freer and more able to express themselves in a sexual way, including their representation on social networking sites and their use of MMS (sexting); and
■ the actions of paedophiles, bullies and stalkers who are freed by anonymity and false identity and an 'exhaustive potential to contact potential victims' (Powell, 2007: 113) to groom, victimise and solicit on the internet.

The approach to e-safety in this area is twofold; it is one of information and of guidance. There needs to be a clear and firm message about acceptable behaviour, reasonable behaviour and an explicit code of conduct. Schools adopting such procedures are more likely to impact upon children's behaviour. The 'acceptable use policy' (AUP) is the response that many schools employ with both pupils and teachers. The AUP, in combination with

Table 5.1 Content, contact and conduct aspects of e-safety

	Commercial	Aggressive	Sexual	Values
Content The learner is subject to the inappropriate activity	The learner needs to be understanding of, and resilient to, advertising, spam, sponsorships and demands for personal information	The learner needs to be resilient to violent/hateful content and know how to deal with it	The learner needs to be resilient to pornographic and unwelcome sexual content	The learner needs to be able to identify bias, racism, misleading information and advice
Contact The learner is a participant in the inappropriate activity	The learner needs to be aware of tracking, harvesting and the protection of personal information	The learner needs to be resilient to being bullied, harassed or stalked and know what action to take in such situations	The learner needs to understand the implications of meeting strangers and being groomed	The learner needs to be resilient to unwelcome persuasions
Conduct The learner is initiating the inappropriate action	The learner must be given clear guidance with regard to illegal downloading, hacking, gambling, financial scams and terrorism and understand the consequences of such actions	The learner must be given clear guidance with regard to bullying or harassing another and understand the consequences of such actions	The learner must be given clear guidance with regard to creating and uploading inappropriate material and understand the consequences of such actions	The learner must be given clear guidance with regard to providing misleading information or advice and plagiarising material

Source: Based on Byron (2008: 16).

classroom-based codes of conduct, are ways in which social mores can impact upon the learners' decision making.

Philosophical motivation/corporate message about the underlying values;

rationale for network and internet access;

advice and instruction for appropriate patterns of use (netiquette);

advice and instruction for expected patterns of use;

declaration of the importance of self-regulation and personal responsibility;

statements regarding legal requirements (including computer misuse, protection of personal data, copyright and obscene materials); and

description of consequences of violating the policy, including punishments and appeal procedures.

Figure 5.2 Essential elements of acceptable use policies

Two years after the publication of the Byron Review, Tanya Byron, at the invitation of the UK government, comments on progress; she confirms the UK as the world leader in child internet safety but advised that 'Government and Industry need to make faster progress in delivery if the UK is to stay ahead of advances in technology' (DCSF, 2010) and identifies the 'Zip it, Block it, Flag it' public awareness raising aimed at parents as a particular success (see Table 5.2). However, there still remains the issue of many mainstream providers of resources and social networking not facilitating fast report mechanisms that would make children feel more secure and give information directly to the law enforcement agencies, such as the UK Child Exploitation and Online Protection Centre – internet safety (CEOP, 2010) and parents condoning children's use of adult social networking sites such as Facebook (under the age of 13 years) and Second Life® (under the age of 18 years).

Table 5.2 'Click Clever Click Safe' campaign, UK Council for Child Internet Safety

Zip It	Block It	Flag It
Keep your personal stuff private and think about what you say or do online	Block people who send nasty messages and don't open unknown links and attachments	Flag up with someone you trust if anything upsets you or if someone asks to meet you offline

E-safety has to be a key consideration of any online educational activity. The impact of that consideration should not be to stop activities but to make those activities as safe as possible without unnecessarily impacting on the pedagogic value. The value of the VLE in providing that safe and secure environment is important. But, because of some of the limitations of the VLE, the value of access to the open internet is also necessary in the education of learners. It is therefore necessary to provide appropriate and repeated information, advice and guidance to learners. Only through each learner's own resilience can they become an independent and safe learners in the online and virtual worlds to which they will be exposed in their education and personal lives.

Activities

- Compare your teaching practice with one of the vignettes and consider how you could enhance teaching and learning by adopting the pedagogic or cybergogic principles.
- Consider how vignettes representing good teaching practice outside of the context of your teaching could be adapted and made usable by you; for example, as a primary school teacher, use a virtual world to explore ideas of travel.
- Considering your own teaching, which aspect of your practice most fully integrates learning technologies? How could a vignette represent your teaching?

References

4Mation (2010). *Granny's Garden*. Barnstaple, UK: 4Mation Educational Resources.

Abd El-Gawad, T. and Woollard, J. (2010). *Embedding Quality in E-learning Systems: A Route to 'Classless Learning'*. Paper presented at the INSPIRE XV e-Learning and Social Responsibility.

Abelson, H. (1982). *Apple Logo*. BYTE/McGraw Hill.

Acorn Computers (1993). *The Horizon Project*. Winchester, UK: Hampshire Microtechnology Centre.

Amey, C. A. (2007). *Primary Teachers' Attitudes to Information and Communication Technology (ICT) in Education*. Southampton, UK: University of Southampton theses.

Anderson, L. W. and Krathwohl, D. R. (2001). *A Taxonomy for Learning, Teaching and Assessing: A Revision of Bloom's Taxonomy of Educational Objectives*. New York: Longman.

Arnold, L., Williams, T. and Thompson, K. (2009). 'Advancing the patchwork text: The development of patchwork media approaches'. *The International Journal of Learning*, (16)5, 151–166.

Askew, M., Brown, M., Rhodes, V., Wiliam, D. and Johnson, D. (1997). *Effective Teachers of Numeracy: Report of a Study Carried Out for the Teacher Training Agency*. London: King's College, University of London.

Atari (2010). *Atari Museum: Historical Notes*. Online. Available HTTP http://www.atarimuseum.com/computers/computers.html (accessed 2 November 2010).

Baby Toys (2010). Online. Available HTTP http://babytoysandtoddlertoys.com/LeapFrogMyPalScout (accessed 2 November 2010).

Bailenson, J. N. and Segovia, K. Y. (2010) 'Virtual doppelgangers: Psychological effects of avatars who ignore their owners'. In Bainbridge W. S. (ed.), *Online Worlds: Convergence of the Real and the Virtual, Human–Computer Interaction Series*. London: Springer-Verlag

Bailenson, J. N. and Yee, N. (2007). 'Virtual interpersonal touch: Haptic interaction and copresence in collaborative virtual environments'. *International Journal of Multimedia Tools and Applications*, 37, 5–14.

Bandura, A. (1977). *Social Learning Theory*. New York: General Learning Press.

Barak, A. and Block, N. (2006). 'Factors related to perceived helpfulness in supporting highly distressed individuals through an online support chat'. *Cyberpsychology and Behaviour*, 9(1), 60–68.

Becta (2010). *Impact of technology.* Coventry, UK: Becta Online. Available HTTP http://www.becta.org.uk/impact.php (accessed 2 November 2010).

Beetham, H. and Sharpe, R. (2007). *Rethinking Pedagogy for a Digital Age.* London: Routledge.

Bernard, R., Abrami, P., Lou, Y., Borokhovski, E., Wade, A., Wozney, L., Wallet, P., Fiset, M. and Huang, B. (2004). 'How does distance education compare with classroom instruction? A meta-analysis of the empirical literature'. *Review of Educational Research,* 74(3), 379–439.

Black, P. and Wiliam, D. (1998a). 'Assessment and classroom learning'. *Assessment in Education,* 5(1), 7–71.

Black, P. and Wiliam, D. (1998b). *Inside the Black Box: Raising Standards Through Classroom Assessment.* Online. Available HTTP http://www.collegenet.co.uk/admin/download/inside%20the%20black%20box_23_doc.pdf (accessed 2 November 2010).

Bloom, B. S. and Krathwohl, D. R. (1956). *Taxonomy of Educational Objective Handbook 1 – Cognitive Domain.* New York: Longman.

Bloome, D., Carter, S. P., Christian, B. M., Otto, S. and Shuart-Faris, N. (2005). *Discourse Analysis and the Study of Classroom Language and Literacy Events: A Microethnographic Perspective.* Mahwah, NJ: Lawrence Erlbaum Associates.

Bolliger, D. U., Supanakorn, S. and Boggs, C. (2010). 'Impact of podcasting on student motivation in the online learning environment'. *Computers and Education,* 55(2), 714–722.

Bono, de, E. (1969). *The Five-Day Course in Thinking.* New York: Basic Books.

Bono, de, E. (1985). *Six Thinking Hats.* Toronto, Canada: Key Porter.

Bono, de, E. (2007). *How to Have Creative Ideas.* London: Vermillion.

Book, B. (2006). *Virtual Worlds: Today and in the Future.* London: British Computer Society. Online. Available HTTP http://www.bcs.org/server.php?show=Con WebDoc.3336 (accessed 2 November 2010).

Boud, D. (2000). 'Sustainable assessment: Rethinking assessment for the learning society'. *Studies in Continuing Education,* 22(2), 151–167.

Boud, D. and Falchikov, N. (2005). 'Redesigning assessment for learning beyond higher education'. *Research and Development in Higher Education,* 28.

Brindley, S. (2002). 'Teaching as professional inquiry: The importance of research and evidence'. In Ellis, V. (ed.), *Teaching and Learning in Secondary Schools.* Exeter, UK: Learning Matters.

Brown, J. S., Collins, A. and Duguid, P. (1989). 'Situated cognition and the culture of learning'. *Educational Researcher,* 18(1), 32–41.

Bruner, J. S. (1966). *Toward a Theory of Instruction.* Cambridge, MA: Harvard University Press.

Bruner, J. S. (1990). *Acts of Meaning.* Cambridge, MA: Harvard University Press.

Bull, J. and McKenna, C. (2004). *Blueprint for Computer-assisted Assessment.* London: RoutledgeFalmer.

Burton, D. and Bartlett, S. (2006). 'Shaping pedagogy from psychological ideas'. In Kassem, D., Mufti, E. and Robinson, J. (eds), *Education Studies: Issues and Critical Perspectives.* Milton Keynes, UK: Open University Press.

Byron, T. (2008). *Safer Children in a Digital World: The Report of the Byron Review.* London: DCSF. Online. Available HTTP http://www.dcsf.gov.uk/byronreview (accessed 2 November 2010).

Carless, D. (2007). 'Learning-oriented assessment: Conceptual bases and practical implications'. *Innovations in Education and Teaching International*, 44(1), 57–66.

Carrier, S. I. and Moulds, L. D. (2003). 'Pedagogy, andragogy, and cybergogy: Exploring best-practice paradigm for online teaching and learning'. Sloan-C 9th International Conference on Asynchronous Learning Networks (ALN) cited in Cronin *et al.*, 2009.

CEOP (2010). *The Child Exploitation and Online Protection Centre* (CEOP). Online. Available HTTP http://www.ceop.gov.uk (accessed 2 November 2010).

Chandler, D. (1984). *Young Learners and the Microcomputer*. Milton Keynes: Open University Press.

Childnet (2005). *Jenny's Story: An Internet safety Resource*. London: Childnet International. Online. Available HTTP http://www.childnet-int.org/jenny (accessed 2 November 2010).

Chowdry, H., Crawford, C. and Goodman, A (2009). *Drivers and Barriers to Educational Success Evidence from the Longitudinal Study of People in England*. London: Institute for Fiscal Studies.

Churches, A. (2009). *Bloom's Digital Taxonomy*. Online. Available HTTP http://edori gami.wikispaces.com/Bloom's+Digital+Taxonomy (accessed 2 November 2010).

Condie, R. and Livingston, K. (2007). 'Blending online learning with traditional approaches: Changing practices'. *British Journal of Educational Technology*, 38(2), 337–348.

Conole, G. (2007). 'Describing learning activities in Beetham and Sharpe'. *Rethinking Pedagogy for a Digital Age*. London: Routledge.

Conole, G. and Oliver, M. (2007). *Contemporary Perspectives in E-Learning Research: Themes, Methods and Impact on Practice*. London: RoutledgeFalmer.

Conole, G., Dyke, M., Oliver, M. and Seale, J. (2004). 'Mapping pedagogy and tools for effective learning design'. *Computers and Education*, 43, 17–33.

Cook, J., White, S., Sharples, M., Sclater, N. and Davis, H. (2006) 'The design of learning technologies'. In G. Conole and M. Oliver, M. (eds). *Learning Technologies – Multiple Perspectives on an Emerging Field* (pp. 55–68). Oxford: Routledge.

Cranmer, S., Selwyn, N. and Potter, J. (2009). 'Exploring primary pupils' experiences and understandings of "e-safety"'. *Journal of Educational Information Technology*, 14, 127–142.

Cronin, J. G. R., McMahon, J. P. and Waldron, M. (2009). 'Critical survey of information technology use in higher education: Blended classrooms'. In C. R. Payne (ed.), *Information Technology and Constructivism in Higher Education: Progressive Learning Frameworks* (pp. 203–215). Hershey, PA: Information Science Reference.

Cuban, L. (2001). *Oversold and Underused: Computers in the Classroom*. London: Harvard University Press.

Cunningham, M. and Harris, S. (2003). *The Ever-open Classroom: Using ICT to Enhance Communication and Learning*. Slough, UK: National Foundation for Educational Research.

Curran, K., Kinney, S. M., Burns, F. and Meredith, G. (2006). 'Scheduled RSS feeds for streaming multimedia to the desktop using RSS enclosures'. *Consumer Communications and Networking Conference 2006*. Las Vegas, NV: IEEE. Online. Available HTTP http://ieeexplore.ieee.org/xpl/freeabs_all.jsp?arnumber=1593029 (accessed 2 November 2010).

Cuthell, J. P. (2002). *Virtual Learning*. Aldershot, UK: Ashgate.

Dale, E. (1969). *Audio-visual Methods in Teaching* (3rd edn). London: Holt, Rinehart and Winston.

Danet, B., Wachenhauser, T., Bechar-Israeli, H., Cividalli, A. and Rosenbaum-Tamari, Y. (1995). 'Curtain time 20:00 GMT: Experiments with virtual theater on internet relay chat'. *Journal of Computer-mediated Communication*, 1(2). Online. Available HTTP http://jcmc.indiana.edu/issues.html (accessed 2 November 2010).

DCSF (2008). *The Assessment for Learning Strategy*. London: Department for Children, Schools and Families.

De Lucia, A., Francese, R., Passero, I. and Tortora, G. (2008). *Supporting Jigsaw-based Collaborative Learning in Second Life*. Online. Available HTTP http://delta4.dmi. unisa.it/francese/pubs/CR_ICALT08_232_delucia.pdf (accessed 2 November 2010).

DfES (2002a). *ImpaCT2 The Impact of Information and Communication Technologies on Pupil Learning and Attainment*. London: Department for Education and Skills.

DfES (2002b). *Key Stage 3 National Strategy Framework for Teaching ICT Capability: Years 7, 8 and 9*. London: Department for Education and Skills.

DfES (2004a). *Key Stage 3 National Strategy ICT Across the Curriculum*. London: Department for Education and Skills.

DfES (2004b). *Progress towards a Unified E-learning Strategy*. London: Department for Education and Skills.

DfES (2004c). *Developing Objective Led Lessons in Mathematics*. London: Department for Education and Schools. Online. Available HTTP http://nationalstrategies.stan-dards.dcsf.gov.uk/downloader/10771718f524991286e7c52db63f4ec3.pdf (accessed 2 November 2010).

DfES (2005). *Working Together: Coaching and Assessment for Learning*. London: Department for Education and Skills. Online. Available HTTP http://nationalstrat egies.standards.dcsf.gov.uk/downloader/bbf4ad0ddfebef6ab1ef24339f48e842.zip (accessed 2 November 2010).

DfES (2006). *Assessment for Learning Guidance for Senior Leaders*. London: Department for Education and Skills.

Donnelly, K. M. and Berge, Z. L. (2006). 'Podcasting: Co-opting MP3 players for education and training purpose'. *Online Journal of Distance Learning Administration*, 9(3). Online. Available HTTP http://www.westga.edu/~distance/ojdla/fall93/ donnelly93.htm (accessed 2 November 2010).

Doyle, D. (2010). 'Immersed in learning: Supporting creative practice in virtual worlds'. *Learning, Media and Technology*, 35(2), 99–110.

Dwyer, D. C., Ringstaff, C. and Sandholtz, J. H. (1990). *Teacher Beliefs and Practices Part I: Patterns of Change The Evolution of Teachers' Instructional Beliefs and Practices in High-Access-to-Technology Classrooms: First–Fourth Year Findings*. Cupertino, CA: Apple Computer Inc.

ECDL (2010). *European Computer Driving Licence*. Online. Available HTTP http:// www.ecdl.com (accessed 2 November 2010).

Edexcel (2010). *Diplomas in Digital Applications*. Online. Available HTTP http://www. edexcel.com/quals/dida (accessed 2 November 2010).

Edwards, A. D. and Westgate, D. P. G. (1994). *Investigating Classroom Talk* (2nd edn). London: Falmer.

Ellis, V. (ed) (2002). *Teaching and Learning in Secondary Schools*. Exeter, UK: Learning Matters.

Ellis, W. D. (1938). *A Source Book of Gestalt Psychology*. New York: Harcourt, Brace and World.

EPPI (2010). *Why is It Important to be Systematic?* London: EPPI-Centre, Institute of Education. Online. Available HTTP http://eppi.ioe.ac.uk/cms/Default.aspx?tabid=69 (accessed 2 November 2010).

Erikson, E. H. (1968). *Identity, Youth and Crisis*. New York: Norton.

Felicia, P. (2011). *International Journal of Game-based Learning*. Hershey, PA: IGI Global.

Finlayson, H., Maxwell, B., Caillau, I. and Tomalin, J. (2006). *Impact of E-learning in Further Education: The Impact on Student Intermediate and End-point Outcomes*. London: Department for Education and Skills. Online. Available HTTP http://www.dfes.gov.uk/research/data/uploadfiles/RR739.pdf (accessed 2 November 2010).

Fose, L. and Mehl, M. (2007). 'Plugging into students' digital DNA five myths prohibiting proper podcasting pedagogy in the new classroom domain MERLOT'. *Journal of Online Learning and Teaching*, 3(3), 277–287.

Freedman, T. (2005). *Every Child Matters: What It Means for the ICT Teacher*. Online. Available HTTP http://www.ictineducation.org (accessed 2 November 2010).

Freegrounds (2010). *Virtual Learning Environment*. Online. Available HTTP http://www.freegrounds-jun.hants.sch.uk/misc/misc/esafety.html (accessed 1 August 2010).

Freeman-longo, R. E. (2000). 'Children, teens, and sex on the internet'. *Sexual Addiction and Compulsivity*, 7(1/2), 75–90.

Freiermuth, M. and Jarrell, D. (2006). 'Willingness to communicate: Can online chat help?'. *International Journal of Applied Linguistics*, 16(2), 189–212.

Freud, S. (1960). *The Ego and the Id*. New York: Norton.

Futurelab (2010). 'Developing the home–school relationship using digital technologies'. Bristol, UK: Futurelab. Online. Available HTTP http://www.futurelab.org.uk/resources/documents/handbooks/home-school_relationships.pdf (accessed 2 November 2010).

Gardner, H. (1983). *Frames of Mind: The Theory of Multiple Intelligences*. New York: Basic Books.

Gardner, H. (2008). *Education, Social Media and Ethics*. Online. Available HTTP http://vimeo.com/2235438 (accessed 2 November 2010).

Gardner, M. and Ward, H. (1999). 'Real-time interactive social environments: A review of BT's Generic Learning platform'. *ALT-J*, 7(3), 17–32.

Garris, R., Ahlers, R. and Driskell, J. (2002). 'Games, motivation and learning: A research and practice model'. *Simulation and Gaming*, 33(4), 441–467.

Gee, J. P. (2003). *What Video Games Have to Teach Us About Learning and Literacy*. New York: Palgrave Macmillan.

Goldberg, L. R. (1993). 'The structure of phenotypic personality traits'. *American Psychologist*, 48, 26–34.

Goleman, D. (2006) *Emotional Intelligence: 10th Anniversary Edition: Why It Can Matter More Than IQ*. New York: Bantam.

GoodPlay Project (2009). *Meeting of Minds: Cross-generational Dialogue on the Ethics of Digital Life*. Cambridge, MA: Project Zero, Harvard Graduate School of Education. Online. Available HTTP http://www.goodworkproject.org/research/digital.htm (accessed 2 November 2010).

Goswami, U. (2008). *Byron Review on the Impact of New Technologies on Children: A Research Literature Review: Child Development*. London: Department for Children,

Schools and Families. Online. Available HTTP http://www.dcsf.gov.uk/byron review/pdfs/Goswami%20Child%20Development%20Literature%20Review%20 for%20the%20Byron%20Review.pdf (accessed 2 November 2010).

Govier, H. (1985). *Posing and Solving Problems with a Micro*. Coventry, UK: MEP.

Grant, D. (2009). *Domesday Preservation Group*. Online. Available HTTP http://www. domesday1986.com (accessed 2 November 2010).

Greenfield, S. (2009). *ID: The Quest for Identity in the 21st Century*. London: Sceptre.

Grigsby, A. (2001). 'Let's chat: Chat rooms in the elementary school'. *Educational Technology and Society*, 4(3).

Gubacs-Collins, K. and Juniu, S. (2009). 'The mobile gymnasium using tablet PCs in physical education'. *Journal of Physical Education, Recreation & Dance*, 80(2), 1–58

Gunawardena, C. N. and McIsaac, M. S. (2004). 'Distance education'. In Jonassen, D. H. and Driscoll, M. P. (eds), *Handbook of Research on Educational Communications and Technology* (pp. 355–395).

Habbo (2010). *Habbo*. Online. Available HTTP http://www.habbo.com (accessed 2 November 2010).

Hallworth, H. J. (1968). 'Educational uses of electronic computers in the United Kingdom'. *Journal International Review of Education*, 14(2), 238–242.

Harden, R. (2006). 'E-learning and all that jazz'. *Medical Teacher*, 28(2), 396.

Harris, P. L., Brown, E., Marriott, C., Whittall, S. and Harmer, S. (1991). 'Monsters, ghosts and witches: Testing the limits of the fantasy–reality distinction in young children'. *British Journal of Developmental Psychology*, 9, 105–123.

Heppell, S. (1993). 'Teacher education, learning and the information generation: The progression and evolution of educational computing against a background of change'. *Journal of Information Technology for Teacher Education*, 2(2), 229–237.

Herring, S. C. (1996). *Computer-mediated Communication: Linguistic, Social and Cross-cultural perspectives*. Amsterdam, Netherlands: Benjamins.

Hope, M. (1986). *The Magic of the Micro: A Resource for Children with Learning Difficulties*. London: Council for Educational Technology.

Hrastinski, S. (2008). 'A study of asynchronous and synchronous e-learning methods discovered that each supports different purposes'. *EDUCAUSE Quarterly*, 31(4). Online. Available HTTP http://www.educause.edu/163445 (accessed 2 November 2010).

Hung, D. and Khine, M. (2006). *Engaged Learning with Emerging Technologies*. Dordrecht, Netherlands: Springer.

Hunsinger, J. and Krotoski, A. (2010). 'Learning and researching in virtual worlds'. *Learning, Media and Technology*, 35(2), 93–97.

Inhelder, B. and Piaget, J. (1958). *The Growth of Logical Thinking from Childhood to Adolescence*. London: Routledge.

ITCOLE (2003). *Innovative Technology for Collaborative Learning and Knowledge Building (ITCOLE) Project*. Online. Available HTTP http://www.euro-cscl.org/site/itcole (accessed 2 November 2010).

Jarvis, P. (2004). *Adult Education and Lifelong Learning: Theory and Practice*. London: RoutledgeFalmer.

JISC (2004). *Effective Practice with e-Learning*. Online. Available HTTP http://www. jisc.ac.uk/media/documents/publications/effectivepracticedigitalage.pdf (accessed 2 November 2010).

JISC (2007). *REAP: Re-engineering Assessment Practices in Scottish Higher Education*.

Online. Available HTTP http://www.jisc.ac.uk/media/documents/programmes/elearningsfc/sfcbookletreap.pdf (accessed 2 November 2010).

John, O. P. and Srivastava, S. (1999). 'The Big Five trait taxonomy: History, measurement and theoretical perspectives'. In Pervin, L. A. and John, O. P. (eds), *Handbook of Personality: Theory and research* (pp. 102–138). New York: Guilford.

Johnson, S. (2005). *Everything Bad is Good for You: How Today's Popular Culture is Actually Making us Smarter*. London: Riverhead.

Jonassen, D. H. and Driscoll, M. P. (2004). *Handbook of Research on Educational Communications and Technology*. London: Routledge.

Jukes, I. (2010). *Understanding the Digital Generation*. Online. Available HTTP http://understandingthedigitalgeneration.com/dvd.cfm (accessed 2 November 2010).

Kapp, K. (2007). *Synchronous Learning Systems: Benchmarks, Best Practices and Real-time Analysis About Real-time Learning* (pp. 139–148). The eLearning Guild, USA.

Kapp, K. M. and O'Driscoll, T. (2007). 'Escape from Flatlands: The emergence of 3D synchronous learning'. *Synchronous Learning Systems: Benchmarks, Best Practices and Real-time analysis about Real-time Learning*. Santa Rosa, CA: e-Learning Guild.

Kapp, K. M. and O'Driscoll, T. (2010). *Learning in 3D: Adding a New Dimension to Enterprise Learning and Collaboration*. San Francisco, CA: Pfeiffer.

Kar2ouche (2010). *Creative Role-play, Picture Making, Storyboarding and Animation*. Online. Available HTTP http://www.immersiveeducation.eu/index.php/kar2ouchepg (accessed 2 November 2010).

Keller, J. M. (1979). 'Motivation and instructional design: A theoretical perspective'. *Journal of Instructional Development*, 2, 26–34.

Keller, J. M. (1999). 'Motivation in cyber learning environments'. *International Journal of Educational Technology*, 1(1), 7–30.

Kelly, B. (2005). 'RSS: More than just news feeds'. *New Review of Information Networking*, 11(2), 219–227.

Kennewell, S. (2001). 'Using affordances and constraints to evaluate the use of information and communications technology in teaching and learning'. *Journal of Information Technology for Teacher Education*, 10(1&2), 101–116.

Kennewell, S., Parkinson, J. and Tanner, H. (2003). *Learning to Teach ICT in the Secondary School*. London: RoutledgeFalmer.

Kennewell, S., Connell, A., Edwards, A., Hammond, M. and Wickens, C. (2007). *A Practical Guide to Teaching ICT in the Secondary School (Routledge Teaching Guides)*. Oxford: Routledge.

Kennewell, S., Tanner, H., Jones, S. and Beauchamp, G. (2008). Analysing the use of interactive technology to implement interactive teaching. *Journal of Computer Assisted Learning*, 24(1), 61–73.

Knowles, M. (1970). *The Modern Practice of Adult Education: Andragogy versus Pedagogy*. New York: Association Press.

Knowles, M. (1980). *The Modern Practice of Adult Education: From Pedagogy to Andragogy*. Englewood Cliffs, NJ: Prentice Hall.

Kodu (2010). *Programming as a Creative Medium*. Online. Available HTTP http://research.microsoft.com/en-us/projects/kodu (accessed 2 November 2010).

Kohlberg, L. (1975). 'The cognitive-developmental approach to moral education'. *Phi Delta Kappan*, 56, 670–677.

Kollias, V. P. and Vosniadou, S. (2002). *Systemic Theory in Classrooms: Results from the CL-Net and the ITCOLE Projects*. Cognitive Science and Educational Technology

Laboratory. National and Kapodistrian University of Athens 2002. Online. Available HTTP http://afscet.asso.fr/resSystemica/Crete02/Kollias.pdf (accessed 2 November 2010).

Kordaki, M. (2005). 'The role of synchronous communication via chat in the formation of e-learning communities'. *Proceedings Book of the 3rd International Conference on Multimedia and Information and Communication Technologies in Education m-ICTE2005.* Online. Available HTTP http://www.formatex.org/micte2006 (accessed 2 November 2010).

Kudlian (2008). *ReTreeval.* Online. Available HTTP http://www.kudlian.net/products/retreeval (accessed 2 November 2010).

Landsberger, H. (1958). *Hawthorne Revisited.* New York: Cornell University Press.

Laurillard, D. (2002). *Rethinking University Teaching: A Framework for the Effective Use of Educational Technology* (2nd edn). London: RoutledgeFalmer.

Lave, J. and Wenger, E. (1991). *Situated Learning: Legitimate Peripheral Participation.* Cambridge: Cambridge University Press.

Linden Lab (2010) Second Life®. Online. Available HTTP http://lindenlab.com (accessed 2 November 2010).

Livingstone, S. and Bober, M. (2005). *UK Children Go Online: Final Report of Key Project Findings.* London: LSE Research. Online. Available HTTP http://eprints.lse.ac.uk/399 (accessed 2 November 2010).

Livingstone, S. and Helsper, E. (2007). 'Taking risks when communicating on the internet: The role of offline social-psychological factors in young people's vulnerability to online risks'. *Information, Communication and Society*, 10(5), 619–643.

Lockhorst, D., Admiraal, W. and Pilot, A. (2010). 'CSCL in teacher training: What learning tasks lead to collaboration?'. *Technology, Pedagogy and Education*, 19(1), 63–78.

Loveless, A. (1995). *The Role of IT: Practical Issues for the Primary Teacher.* London: Cassell.

Loveless, A. and Ellis, V. (2001). *ICT Pedagogy and the Curriculum – Subject to Change.* London: Routledge.

Loveless, A., DeVoogd, G. L. and Bohlin, R. M. (2001). 'Something old, something new ... Is pedagogy affected by ICT?'. In A. Loveless and V. Ellis (eds), *ICT Pedagogy and the Curriculum – Subject to Change.* London: Routledge.

Ma, R. (1996). 'Computer-mediated conversations as a new dimension of intercultural communication between East Asian and North American college students'. In S. C. Herring (ed.), *Computer-mediated Communication: Linguistic, Social and Cross-cultural Perspectives* (pp. 173–185).

Maier, P. and Warren, A. (2002). *Integrating Technology in Learning and Teaching: A Practical Guide for Educators.* London: Kogan Page.

Malaby, T. (2007). 'Contriving constraints (the gameness of Second Life and the persistence of scarcity). *Innovations*, 2(3), 62–67.

Malinowski, B. (1923). 'The problem of meaning in primitive languages'. In C. K. Ogden and I. A. Richards (eds), *The Meaning of Meaning* (pp. 146–152). London: Routledge.

Mallan, K., Foth, M., Greenaway, R. and Young, G. T. (2010) 'Serious playground: Using Second Life to engage high school students in urban planning'. *Learning, Media and Technology*, 35(2), 203–225.

Markle, S. (1969). *Good Frames and Bad*, New York: Wiley.

Martínez, A., Dimitriadisb, Y., Rubiac, B., Gómezb, E. and de la Fuentea, P. (2003). 'Documenting collaborative interactions: Issues and approaches'. *Computers and Education*, 41(4), 353–368.

Maslow, A. H. (1943). 'A theory of human motivation'. *Psychological Review*, 50, 370–396.

Mayes, T. and Fowler, C. J. H. (1999). 'Learning technology and usability: A framework for understanding courseware'. *Interacting with Computers*, 11, 485–497. Online. Available HTTP http://www2.napier.ac.uk/transform/Digital_Literacy. pdf (accessed 2 November 2010).

Mayes, T. and de Freitas, S. (2007). 'Learning and e-learning: The role of theory'. In H. Beetham and R. Sharpe (eds), *Rethinking Pedagogy for a Digital Age: Designing and Delivering e-Learning* (pp. 13–23). Abingdon, UK: Routledge.

Meadows, M. S. (2008). *I, Avatar: The Culture and Consequences of Having a Second Life*. Berkeley, CA: New Riders.

Medwell, J., Poulson, L., Avramidis, E., Fox, E. and Wray, D. (2001). 'The theoretical beliefs of effective teachers of literacy in primary schools: An exploratory study of orientations to reading and writing'. *Research Papers in Education*, 16(3), 271–292.

Mercer, N., Littleton, K. and Wegerif, R. (2004). 'Methods for studying the processes of interaction and collaborative activity in computer-based educational activities'. *Technology, Pedagogy and Education*, 13(2), 193–209.

Meredith, M. D. and Briggs, B. I. (1982). *Bigtrak Plus. Case Study 3 (Microelectronics Education Programme)*. London: Council for Educational Technology.

Meyer, J. H. F. and Land, R. (2003). *Threshold Concepts and Troublesome Knowledge: Linkages to Ways of Thinking and Practising*. Online. Available HTTP http://www. tla.ed.ac.uk/etl/docs/ETLreport4.pdf (accessed 2 November 2010).

Meyer, J. H. F. and Land, R. (eds.) (2006). *Overcoming Barriers to Student Understanding: Threshold Concepts and Troublesome Knowledge*. London: Routledge.

Michael, M. (2000). *Reconnecting Culture, Technology and Nature: From Society to Heterogeneity*. London: Routledge.

Mitchell, P. D. (1997). 'The impact of educational technology: A radical reappraisal of research methods'. *ALT-J*, 5(1), 48–54.

Mohamad, M. and Woollard, J. (2008). 'Why does Malaysia need to consider mobile technologies? A review of current practices to support teaching and learning with school-age children'. *Mobile Learning and Edutainment Conference 2008*. Kuala Lumpur, Malaysia, Malaysia 20–21 November. Online. Available HTTP http:// eprints.soton.ac.uk/52455 (accessed 2 November 2010).

Mohamad, M. and Woollard, J. (2009). 'English language learning through mobile technology in Malaysian schools: An implementation strategy'. *International Conference on E-learning*. Kuala Lumpur, Malaysia, 1–2 December. Online. Available HTTP http://eprints.soton.ac.uk/79366 (accessed 2 November 2010).

Moore, K. and Pflugfelder, E. H. (2010) 'On being bored and lost (in virtuality)'. *Learning, Media and Technology*, 35(2), 249–253.

Mortimer, P. (1999). *Understanding Pedagogy and Its Impact on Learning*. London: Chapman.

Nonnecke, B. and Preece, J. (2000). 'Silent participants: Getting to know lurkers better?'. In *From Usenet to CoWebs* (pp. 110–132). Online. Available HTTP http://www.cis.uoguelph.ca/~nonnecke/research/silentparticipants.pdf (accessed 2 November 2010).

North, M. and McKeown, S. (2005). *Meeting SEN in the Curriculum ICT*. London: David Fulton.

OCR (2010) *OCR Nationals (for 2010)*. Online. Available HTTP http://www.ocr.org.uk/qualifications/type/nationals_2010 (accessed 2 November 2010).

O'Driscoll, T. (2007). *Learning Matters*. Online. Available HTTP http://wadatripp.wordpress.com/2007/10/22/escaping-flatlandlearning-via-the-first-person-inter-face (accessed 2 November 2010).

Offir, B. and Lev, Y. (1999). 'Teacher–learner interaction in the process of operating DL (distance learning) systems'. *Educational Media International*, 36(2), 132–136.

Offir, B., Leva, Y. and Bezalela, R. (2008). 'Surface and deep learning processes in distance education: Synchronous versus asynchronous systems'. *Computers and Education*, 51(3), 1172–1183.

Oliver, R. and McLaughlin, C. (1996). *An Investigation of the Nature and Forms of Interaction in Live Interactive Television, ERIC Document ED396738*. Online. Available HTTP http://www.eric.ed.gov (accessed 2 November 2010).

OPSI (1988). *Education Reform Act 1988*. London: Office for Public Sector Information.

Oswell, D. (1998). 'The place of "childhood" in internet content regulation'. *International Journal of Cultural Studies*, 1(2), 271–291.

Papert, S. A. (1980). *Mindstorms: Children, Computers and Powerful Ideas*. Boston, MA: Basic Books.

Patterson, L. J. (2006). 'The technology underlying podcasts'. *Computer*, 39(10), 103–105.

Payne, C. R. (2009). *Information Technology and Constructivism in Higher Education: Progressive Learning Frameworks*. New York: Information Science Reference.

Pearson (2009). *SuccessMaker®*. Online. Available HTTP http://www.pearsonschool.com/index.cfm?locator=PSZdXp (accessed 2 November 2010).

Perrenoud, P. (1998). 'From formative evaluation to a controlled regulation of learning processes: Towards a wider conceptual field'. *Assessment in Education: Principles, Policy and Practice*, 5(1), 85–102.

Piaget, J. (1929/1964). *The Child's Conception of the World*. London: Routledge.

Piper, G. (2000). *The Use of Roamer as a Constructivist Tool in Early Learning*. Online. Available HTTP http://www.pgce.soton.ac.uk/ict/roamer (accessed 2 November 2010).

Potter, J. (2010). *Podcast in Futurelab Harnessing Technology Series 2 Episode 5: Technology and Primary Education*. Bristol, UK: Futurelab. Online. Available HTTP http://media.futurelab.org.uk/podcasts/becta_talks/primary_education/ (accessed August 1, 2010).

Powell, A. (2007). *Paedophiles, Child Abuse and the Internet*. Oxford: Radcliffe.

Powell, S., Tindal, I. and Millwood, R. (2008). 'Personalized learning and the Ultraversity experience'. *Interactive Learning Environments*, 16(1), 63–81.

Prensky, M. (2001a). 'Digital native, digital immigrants'. *On the Horizon*, 9(5). Online. Available HTTP http://marcprensky.com/writing (accessed 2 November 2010).

Prensky, M. (2001b). 'Digital native, digital immigrants Part II: Do they really think differently?'. *On the Horizon*, 9(6). Online. Available HTTP http://marcprensky.com/writing (accessed 2 November 2010).

Prensky, M. (2001c). *Why Games Engage Us: Digital Game-based Learning*. New York: McGraw-Hill.

Pritchard, A. (2005). *Ways of Learning*. London: David Fulton.

Pritchard, A. (2009). *Ways of Learning* (2nd edn). London: Routledge.

Pritchard, A. and Woollard, J. (2010). *Psychology for the Classroom: Constructivism and Social Learning*. Oxford: Routledge David Fulton.

QCA (1999). *History. The National Curriculum for England. Key Stages 1–3*. London: Qualifications and Curriculum Authority.

QCDA (2007). *PSHE: Personal Wellbeing. The National Curriculum Online*. London: Qualifications and Curriculum Development Agency.

REAP (2007). *Re-engineering Assessment Practices*. Online. Available HTTP http://www.reap.ac.uk/public/Misc/REAPFlyer.pdf (accessed 2 November 2010).

Richards, C. (2003). 'Chatrooms in the classroom'. *InteracTive*, 47, 23–25. Birmingham, UK: Questions Publishing.

Richards, C. (2009). *How Useful Are Bounded Online Chat Rooms as a Source of Pastoral Support in a Sixth-form College?* University of Southampton, School of Education, Doctoral Thesis, 281 pp. Online. Available HTTP http://eprints.soton.ac.uk/66451/ (accessed 2 November 2010).

Robertson, J. (1998). 'Paradise Lost: Children, multimedia and the myth of inter-activity'. *Journal of Computer Assisted Learning*, 14(1), 31–39.

Rogan, A., Harth, A. and Breslin, J. G. (2005). 'Podcast pinpointer: A multimedia semantic web application'. *Integration of Knowledge, Semantics and Digital Media Technology*. The 2nd European Workshop on the (Ref. No. 2005/11099), IEEE.

Rogers, E. M. (1983). *Diffusion of Innovation* (3rd edn). New York: The Free Press.

Rymaszewski, M., Au, W. J., Ondrejka, C., Platel, R., Van Gorden, S., Cézanne, J., Cézanne, P., Batstone-Cunningham, B., Krotoski, A., Trollop, C. and Rossignol, J. (2008). *Second Life: The Official Guide* (2nd edn). Indianapolis, IN: Wiley.

Salmon, G. (2000). *E-moderating: The Key to Teaching and Learning Online*. London: Kogan Page.

Salovey, P. and Mayer, J. (1994). *Emotional Intelligence, Imagination, Cognition and Personality*, 9, 185–211.

Schroeder, R. and Axelsson, A.-S. (2006). *Avatars at Work and Play: Collaboration and Interaction in Shared Virtual Environments (Computer Supported Cooperative Work)*. Dordrecht, Netherlands: Springer.

Scoggins, J. and Winter, R. (1999). 'The patchwork text: A coursework format for education as critical understanding'. *Teaching in Higher Education*, 4(4), 485–500.

Scopes, L. J. M. (2009). *Learning Archetypes as Tools of Cybergogy for a 3D Educational Landscape: A Structure for eTeaching in Second Life*. Southampton, UK: University of Southampton. Online. Available HTTP http://eprints.soton.ac.uk/66169 (accessed 2 November 2010).

Scrimshaw, P. (1993). *Language, Classrooms and Computers*. London: Routledge.

Segovia, K. Y. and Bailenson, J. N. (2009). 'Virtually true: Children's acquisition of false memories in virtual reality'. *Media Psychology*, 12, 371–393.

Selwyn, N., Potter, J. and Cranmer, S. (2009). 'Primary pupils' use of information and communication technologies at school and home'. *British Journal of Educational Technology*, 40(5), 919–932.

Shen, R. M., Wang, M. J., Gao, W. P., Novak, D. and Tang, L. (2009). 'Mobile Learning in a large blended computer science classroom: System function, pedagogies, and their impact on learning'. *IEEE Transactions on Education*, 52(4), 538–546.

Sherston (2010). *The Model Shop*. Sherston, UK: Sherston. Online. Available HTTP http://shop.sherston.com/sherston/mosh-mlt-cdrm-1.html (accessed 2 November 2010).

Shortis, T. (2001). *The Language of ICT*. London: Routledge.

Shulman, L. S. (1986). 'Those who understand: Knowledge growth in teaching'. *Educational Researcher*, 15, 4–14.

Skinner, B. F. (1948). *Walden Two*. New York: Macmillan.

Skinner, B. F. (1954). 'The science of learning and the art of teaching'. *Harvard Educational Review*, 24(1), 86–97.

Skinner, B. F. (1968). *The Technology of Teaching*. New York: Appleton-Century-Crofts.

Smith, H. J., Higgins, S., Wall, K. and Miller, J. (2005). 'Interactive whiteboards: Boon or bandwagon? A critical review of the literature'. *Journal of Computer Assisted Learning*, 21(2), 91–101.

Somekh, B. (2007). *Pedagogy and Learning with ICT: Researching the Art of Innovation*. London: Routledge.

Somekh, B. and Pearson, M. (2002). *The PELRS Project*. Manchester, UK: Manchester Metropolitan University. Online. Available HTTP http://www.esri.mmu.ac.uk/resprojects/pelrs (accessed 2 November 2010).

Somekh, B. and Pearson, M. (2006). *The PELRS Project Summary of Research Findings*. Manchester, UK: Manchester Metropolitan University. Online. Available HTTP http://www.esri.mmu.ac.uk/resprojects/pelrs (accessed 2 November 2010).

Somekh, B., Underwood, J., Convery, A., Dillon, G., Jarvis, J., Lewin, C., Mavers, D., Saxon, D., Sing, S., Steadman, S., Twining, P. and Woodrow, D. (2007). *Final Report of the Evaluation of the ICT Test Bed Project*. Coventry, UK: Becta.

Spector, J. M. and Merrill, M. D. (eds). (2008). 'Effective, efficient, and engaging (E3): Learning in the digital era'. *Distance Education*, 29, 2.

Squires, D. and McDougall, A. (1994). *Choosing and Using Educational Software*. Sussex, UK: Falmer Press.

Stephenson, N. (1992). *Snow Crash*. London: Penguin.

Straker, A. (1989). *Children Using Computers*. Oxford: Basil Blackwell.

Tansley, A. G. (1920). *The New Psychology and Its Relation to Life*. London: Allen & Unwin.

TDA (2008). *Professional Standards for Qualified Teacher Status and Requirements for Initial Teacher Training*. London: The Training and Development Agency for Schools. Online. Available HTTP http://www.tda.gov.uk/qts (accessed 2 November 2010).

Times Online (2009). Online. Available HTTP http://www.timesOnline.co.uk/tol/news/world/us_and_americas/article6460962.ece (accessed 2 November 2010).

Turkle, S. (1984). *The Second Self: Computers and the Human Spirit*. New York: Simon & Schuster.

Turner-Bisset, R. (2001). *Expert Teaching*. London: Fulton.

Twining, P. (2002). *ICT in Schools: Estimating the Level of Investment Report No: 02*. MeD8 Online. Available HTTP http://www. med8. info/docs/meD8_02-01.pdf (accessed 2 November 2010).

US DoE (2009) *Evaluation of Evidence-based Practices in Online Learning: A Meta-analysis and Review of Online Learning Studies*. Washington, DC: US Department of Education, Office of Planning, Evaluation, and Policy Development.

Valient (2010). *Roamer Discovery at Every Turn*. Online. Available HTTP http://www. valiant-technology.com/uk/pages/roamer_home.php?cat=1&1 (accessed 2 November 2010).

Vygotsky, L. S. (1962). *Thought and Language*. Cambridge, MA: MIT Press.

Vygotsky, L. S. (1978). *Mind in Society*, Cambridge, MA: Harvard University Press.

Wang, M. and Kang, M. (2006). 'Cybergogy for engaged learning: A framework for creating learner engagement through information and communication technology'. In D. Hung and M. S. Kline (eds), *Engaged Learning with Emerging Technologies*. Dordrecht, Netherlands: Springer.

Wang, M. J. (2007). 'Designing online courses that effectively engage learners from diverse cultural backgrounds'. *British Journal of Educational Technology*, 38(2), 294–311.

Wang, M., Shen, R., Novak, D. and Pan, X. (2009). 'The impact of mobile learning on students' learning behaviours and performance: Report from a large blended classroom'. *British Journal of Educational Technology*, 40(4), 673–695.

Wenger, E. (1998). *Communities of Practice: Learning, Meaning, and Identity*. Cambridge: Cambridge University Press.

Wenger, E. (2006). *Communities of Practice*. Online. Available HTTP http://www. ewenger.com/theory (accessed 2 November 2010).

Wenger, E., McDermott, R. and Snyder, W. (2002). *Cultivating Communities of Practice: A Guide to Managing Knowledge*. Boston, MA: Harvard Business School Press.

Wenger, E., White, N. and Smith, J. (2009). *Digital Habitats Stewarding Technology for Communities*. Cambridge, MA: CPsquare Press.

Whitty, C. M. (2003). 'Cyber-flirting: Playing at love on the internet'. *Theory and Psychology*, 13, 339–357.

Whitty, C. M. and Joinson, A. (2008). *Truth, Lies and Trust on the Internet*. London: Routledge.

Wickens, C. (2007). 'Creativity'. In Kennewell *et al.* (eds), *A Practical Guide to Teaching ICT in the Secondary School*.

Williams, A. (2003). 'Using Integrated Learning Systems to support students with learning difficulties in a comprehensive school'. *British Journal of Learning Support*, 16(4), 174–178.

Williams, D., Wilson, K., Richardson, A., Tuson, J. and Coles, L. (1998). *Teachers' ICT Skills and Knowledge Needs: Final Report to SOEID*. Aberdeen, UK: The School of Information and Media, Faculty of Management, The Robert Gordon University.

Winter, R. (2003). 'Contextualizing the patchwork text: Addressing problems of coursework assessment in higher education'. *Innovations in Education and Teaching International*, 40(2), 112–122.

Wood, D. (1998). *The UK ILS Evaluations Final Report*. Coventry, UK: British Educational Communications and Technology Agency.

Woollard, J. (2004). *The Rôle of Metaphor in the Teaching of Computing: Towards a Taxonomy of Pedagogic Content Knowledge*. Southampton, UK: University of Southampton. Online. Available HTTP http://eprints.soton.ac.uk/11227 (accessed 2 November 2010).

Woollard, J. (2007a). *Learning and Teaching Using ICT in Secondary Schools (Achieving QTS)*. Exeter, UK: Learning Matters.

Woollard, J. (2007b). 'Prediction'. In Kennewell *et al.*, *A Practical Guide to Teaching ICT in the Secondary School*.

Woollard, J. (2010). *Psychology for the Classroom: Behaviourism*. Oxford: Routledge.

Woollard, J. and Scopes, L. (2010). *Review of the Second Encounter with Second Life Online*. Online. Available HTTP http://www.pgce.soton.ac.uk/IT/Research/ Second Life/SLevalreport2.pdf (accessed 2 November 2010).

Woollard, J., Wickens, C. A., Powell, K. and Russell, T. (2007a). *E-safety: Evaluation of Key Stage 3 Materials for Initial Teacher Education*. London: Childnet International. Online. Available HTTP http://www.childnet-int.org/kia/traineeteachers/about. aspx (accessed 2 November 2010).

Woollard, J., Wickens, C. A., Powell, K. and Russell, T. (2007b). *E-safety: Evaluation of Key Stage 3 Materials for Initial Teacher Education: Executive Summary*. London: Childnet International. Online. Available HTTP http://www.childnet-int.org/ downloads/exec_sum.pdf (accessed 2 November 2010).

Woollard, J., Wickens, C. A., Powell, K. and Russell, T. (2009). 'Evaluation of e-safety materials for initial teacher training: can "Jenny's Story" make a difference?'. *Technology, Pedagogy and Education*, 18(2), 187–200.

Yee, N. (2006). 'The psychology of MMORPGs: Emotional investment, motivations, relationship formation, and problematic usage'. In R. Schroeder and A.-S. Axelsson (eds), *Avatars at Work and Play: Collaboration and Interaction in Shared Virtual Environments*.

Yero, J. L. (2002). *Teaching in Mind: How Teacher Thinking Shapes Education*. Hamilton, GA: Mindflight.

Young, M., Schrader, P. G. and Zheng, D. (2006). 'MMOGs as learning environments: An ecological journey into Quest Atlantis and The Sims Online'. *Innovate Journal of Online Education*, (2)4.

Zhang, D., Zhou, L., Briggs, R. O. and Nunamaker, J. F. (2006). 'Instructional video in e-learning: Assessing the impact of interactive video on learning effectiveness'. *Information and Management*, 43(1), 15–27. Cited in (US DoE, 2009: 40).

Zimmerman, B. J. and Schunk, D. H. (2011). *Handbook of Self-regulation of Learning and Performance*. London: Routledge.

Zins, J., Bloodworth, M., Weissberg, R. and Walberg, H. (2004). 'The scientific base linking social and emotional learning to school success'. In *Building Academic Success on Social and Emotional Learning: What Does the Research Say?*. Teachers College, Columbia University. Online. Available HTTP http://www.casel.org/downloads/ T3053c01.pdf (accessed 2 November 2010).

Zurbriggen, E. L., Collings, R. L., Lamb, S., Roberts, T.-A., Tolman, D. L., Ward, L. M. and Blake, J. (2007). *Report of the APA Task Force on the Sexualisation of Girls*. Washington, DC: American Psychological Association. Cited in Byron, 2008: 51. Online. Available HTTP http://www.apa.org/pi/wpo/sexualizationrep.pdf (accessed 2 November 2010).

Index

Note: page numbers in **bold** refer to illustrations.

3D immersive (3Di) 7, 12, 57, 103, 106, 109; *see also* virtual worlds

Abd El-Gawad 86
action engagement 74
affordances 6, 15, 36; of virtual worlds 92, 103; of VLEs 86
andragogy 11–13, 67
assessment 7, 21, 25, 72, 73, 82, 87, **88**, 101–3, 105–6; ipsative **88**; peer 28, 99
attitudes 6; e-learning 10, 17; e-safety 37–9
authoring 106
avatar 58–63; programming **77**
avatar touching 65

BASIC 9
BBC Microcomputer 8, 72
Becta 32
behaviourism 14, 52–3, 65, 69, 73, 96
belief 21, 70–1
'Big Five' 61, 64
Bigtrak 8
blended learning 3, 21, 24
Bloom, B. S. 6, 101
Bloom's Taxonomy 6
Bono, de, E. 78, **79**, 80–1

Bruner, J. S. 29, 75
Byron, T. 5–6, 41, 114, 116

camaraderie 96
cap of hearing 60, 115
CEOP 117
Childnet 38, 114
cognitive aspects of e-learning 23
cognitive development 17, 39, 45–6, 49
cognitive domain 90, 104, 112
cognitive engagement 28, 33, 35, 75
cognitive overload 86
cognitive skills 6, 39
cognitive stages **46**, 61
cognitivism 14, **15**, 66, 69, 96
collaborative learning 13, 15, 21, **23**, 24, **25**, 54, **56**; in-world 92, 105, 113; on-line 83, 97 103; teacher–learner 68
communities of practice 15, 54
computer-mediated learning (CMC) 99
Conole, G. 10, 54, 68–9
constructionism 66, 76, 96
constructivism **15**, **23**, 28, 31, 46
creativity 9, 33, **64**, **77**, 78, 80
cyber-bullying 39, 40

cybergogy 12–13, **56**, 56–8, 90–2, **91**, 104–6
cyberspace 3, 10, 56

Dale, E. **75**
dexterity 56, 105, 109
dextrous 90, 104, 112
digital divide 30, 42
digital immigrants *see* digital natives
digital natives 4–5, 14
domain affective 53, 73; community of practice 55; cybergogy 55, **57**, 90, 92, **93**, 104, 112; *see also* 'Big Five'

e-learning, definition 2–4
e-safety 37–43, 97
ECDL 10
Ego 41, **60**, 60–1, 78, 115; egocentrism 48
emotion 48, 54, 72, 74, **79**, 90, **91**, **93**
emotional engagement 48, 54, 72; *see also* immersion
emotional intelligence 38
engagement **23**, **27**, 28, 33, 72, 86; learner 106; *see also* action engagement; immersion

feedback 31–2, 41, 54, 72, 74, 87, **88**, 109 (*also see* immediacy); peer 25, 28, 102
Freedman, T. 72
Freud 59–60, 78, 115
functionality 6, 79, 85
FutureLab 33

games 5, 33, 41, 71, 74; authoring of 106; excessive use of 6, 40, 48; MMORPG 7, 41; role playing 7; video 39, 40, 41; *see also* immediacy
Gardner, H. 14, 61
Gestalt 50, 78
Govier, H. 9
Granny's Garden 72
Grass 9

Heppell, S. 9

ICT Test Bed 1
Id *see* Ego
immediacy 11, 67, 69, 73
immersion 12, **56**, 104, 111; *see also* 3D immersive (3Di); emotional engagement
ImpaCT2 1, 30, 32
individualised *see* personalisation
inquiry arousal 35
intelligence 5, 14–15, **91**
interactive whiteboards 32, 46, 90, 96
ipsative assessment **88**

Jarvis, P. 75

Kennewell, S. 6, 10, 69
Kholberg, L. 61
Knowles, M. 12

lateral thinking 65, 78, 80–1
Laurillard, D. 54, **84**
learner-centeredness *see* personalisation
learning cycle 74, 82
learning theory *see* behaviourism; cognitivism; constructivism; social constructivism
lifelong learning 103, 107
Linden Lab 11, 58
Loveless, A. 69–70

mapping *see* visualisation
Maslow, A. H. 15, 59
Mayes, T. 82
Meadows, M. 61, 114
Meredith, M. 8
mindstorms *see* Papert, S. A.
mindtools 21, 66, 75–7, 96, 108
Mohamad, M. 11
morals 38–9; avatar 61; in behaviourism 52; development 61; guidance 17, 40
motivation 15, 17, 21, 32, 35, 41, 71
MULCH **46**, 47

Newman College 9

OCEAN 64
off-task 98–9

Papert, S. A. 8, 76
patchwork **84**, 102–3
PCK 70
pedagogic content knowledge
    see PCK
pedagogy 11–14, 32–3, 67, **68**;
    behaviourist 52; *see also* andragogy;
    cybergogy
PELRS 32–34
peregrination 11, 56, 58, 59, 105, 112
personalisation 3, 7, 17, 59, 84, 101
personality 5, 41, 58; *see also* 'Big Five'
Piaget, J. 45–52, **46**, 61
PLONE 101
prediction 51, 80
Prensky, M. 4–5, 74
Pritchard, A. ix, 12

quiz 73, 87, **88**, **89**, 90, 106–9

regulation of learning 15, 99–100
resilience 37, 79, 115, 118
ROAMER **46**, 47–8

Salmon, G. 15, 29, 54–6, **56**
satisfaction 41

scaffold 76, 86, 111
Scopes, L. 55–6
Scrimshaw, P. 9
Selwyn, N 42–3
Shulman, L. 86
situated learning 11, 75, 101–2
Skinner, B. F. 47, 53, 54
social conditioning 84
social constructivism 15, **27**, 96
social engagement 12, 17, **27**, 71
social interaction 3, 12, **23**, 69, 84–6,
    97–9
social justice 7, 41, 102
social networking 15, 33, 40, 55, 92,
    99, 117
socialisation 55–6
Somekh, B. 1
Straker, A. 8–9, 70–71
synchronicity 21, 23, 26, 78

task analysis 14, 53
Turkle, S. 9
Turner-Bissett, R. 15, 27, 70
Twitter™ 3, 7, 22

virtual worlds 7, 11, 12, 55–8;
    assessment in 105–6
visualisations 76, 77, **83**, 96
Vygotsky, L. S. 28, 35, 106

Wenger, E. 54–5, 75, 102

Psychology for the Classroom: Constructivism and Social Learning

Psychology for the Classroom Series

Alan Pritchard, University of Warwick Institute of Education
John Woollard, University of Southampton School of Education

Psychology for the Classroom: Constructivism and Social Learning provides a lively introduction to the much-debated topics of talk and group collaboration in classrooms and the development of interactive approaches to teaching. The authors provide a background to research in constructivist and social learning theory, offering a broad and practical analysis which focuses on contemporary issues and strategies. Throughout the book, theory is linked with its practical implications for everyday teaching and learning. Chapters incorporate:

* the history of constructivist and social learning theory and key thinkers;
* pedagogical implications;
* practical strategies for the classroom.

Case studies and vignettes demonstrating best practice are used throughout the text, illustrating how monitored collaboration between learners can result in an effective learning environment where targets are met. Essential reading for practising teachers and students, this book is a valuable guide for those looking to provide effective teaching and learning within a constructivist framework.

978-0-415-49480-9
120 pp
PB: £17.99 HB: £75.00
Available: April 2010

For more information and to order a copy visit
www.routledge.com/9780415494809

Available from all good bookshops

Ways of Learning

Learning Theories and Learning
Styles in the Classroom

Second edition

Alan Pritchard, University of
Warwick Institute of Education

Teachers are good at providing excellent opportunities for allowing
children's learning to progress. Often, without fully understanding
the reasons why, teachers encourage learning in their charges which
works well, and is a good approach at a particular time with a
particular child or group of children. With greater insight into what
is currently known about the processes of learning and about
individual learning preferences, teachers are able to provide even
better learning situations which are more likely to lead to effective
learning. This book seeks to provide details which teachers can
make use of in their planning and teaching in order to supply better
opportunities for effective and lasting learning.

The first edition of this book has been used widely and has now
been revised to include updated information in the existing chapters
as well as a new chapter which covers the area of learning
difficulties and special educational needs.

978-0-415-46608-0
124 pp
PB: £17.99
Available: October 2008

For more information and to order a copy visit
www.routledge.com/9780415466080

Available from all good bookshops